T0270002

SIMON NYE

Simon Nye's writing encompasses translations, novels, television sitcoms and drama, adaptations, animation and film. He was a translator before turning to fiction, adapting his two novels *Men Behaving Badly* and *Wideboy* for the small screen. He had a series on all four main terrestrial TV channels in one year, and has won a BAFTA for *Just William*.

Other television series include *The Larkins*, *The Durrells*, an episode of *Doctor Who*, *Hardware*, *Wild West*, *Beast*, *How Do You Want Me*, *Is it Legal?* and *Frank Stubbs*.

TV movies include *Tommy Cooper: Not Like That, Like This*, *My Family and Other Animals*, *Open Wide*, *Tunnel of Love*, *True Love*, and four TV pantomimes.

He has translated the plays *Don Juan* (Sheffield Crucible), and *Accidental Death of an Anarchist* (Donmar).

Simon spent several happy years working in theatre box offices, and now co-runs TV production company Genial Productions. He is married to Claudia, has four children, and lives in London.

Simon Nye

THE
CROWN JEWELS

A Play Based on Real Events

NICK HERN BOOKS

London

www.nickhernbooks.co.uk

A Nick Hern Book

The Crown Jewels first published in Great Britain as a paperback original in 2023 by Nick Hern Books Limited, The Glasshouse, 49a Goldhawk Road, London W12 8QP

The Crown Jewels copyright © 2023 Simon Nye
Song lyrics copyright © 2023 Simon Nye and Grant Olding
(Grant Olding's Music and Lyrics published by Air-Edel Associates Ltd.)

Simon Nye has asserted his right to be identified as the author of this work

Cover artwork by Feast Creative

Designed and typeset by Nick Hern Books, London
Printed in Great Britain by Mimeo Ltd, Huntingdon, Cambridgeshire PE29 6XX

A CIP catalogue record for this book is available from the British Library

ISBN 978 1 83904 245 4

www.nickhernbooks.co.uk/environmental-policy

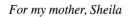

For my mother, Sheila

The Crown Jewels was first performed at the Garrick Theatre, London, on 7 July 2023, produced by Simon Friend. The cast was as follows:

CHARLES II/TALBOT EDWARDS	Al Murray
MRS EDWARDS/FRENCH NOBLEWOMAN	Mel Giedroyc
ELIZABETH EDWARDS/LADY OF THE BEDCHAMBER	Carrie Hope Fletcher
COLONEL BLOOD	Aidan McArdle
CAPTAIN PERROT/TOURIST	Neil Morrissey
WYTHE EDWARDS/FOOTMAN	Adonis Siddique
TOM BLOOD JNR/SUITOR	Joe Thomas
JENNY BLAINE/JAILER	Tanvi Virmani
FOOTMEN/COVERS	Emma Bown
	Kieran Brown
	Ryan Lane
	Dedun Omole
Director	Sean Foley
Set and Costume Designer	Michael Taylor
Lighting Designer	Natasha Chivers
Sound Designer	Andy Graham
Composer	Grant Olding
Song Lyrics	Simon Nye and Grant Olding
Production Manager	Damian Partington
Costume Supervisor	Hilary Lewis
Props Supervisor	Kate Dowling for Propworks
Associate Director	Dewi Johnson
Associate Lighting Designer and Programmer	Marc Polimeni
Fight Director	Alison De Burgh
Musical Director	Tarek Merchant

Choreographer	Lizzi Gee
Dialect Coach	Majella Hurley
Company Stage Manager	Sally Hughes
Deputy Stage Manager	Olivia Kerslake
Assistant Stage Manager/Book Cover	Frances Howell
Head of Wardrobe	Samantha Gray
Head of Wigs, Hair and Make-up	Kadine Watson-Thompson

Characters

KING CHARLES II, *sharp, lusty, ruthless*
LADY OF THE BEDCHAMBER, *game*
FRENCH NOBLEWOMAN, *very French*
FOOTMAN, *personable and bright*
COLONEL THOMAS BLOOD, *charismatic, mercurial Irishman*
TOM BLOOD JNR, *Blood's son, decent, not always the brightest*
JENNY BLAINE, *ballsy youthful actress, keen to showcase her skills*
CAPTAIN ROBERT PERROT, *hothead, ex-preacher, relentlessly angry*
TALBOT EDWARDS, *custodian, old soldier, survivor*
MRS EDWARDS, *good-hearted, industrious*
ELIZABETH EDWARDS, *daughter, emotional*
WYTHE EDWARDS, *son, a fearless, bouncy soldier*
JAILER, *runs a tight jail, loves a celebrity criminal*
TOURIST, *foppish royalist*
SUITOR, *handsome military man*

Suggested Doubling

TALBOT EDWARDS/CHARLES II

MRS EDWARDS/FRENCH NOBLEWOMAN

ELIZABETH EDWARDS/LADY OF THE BEDCHAMBER

WYTHE EDWARDS/FOOTMAN

JAILER/JENNY

TOURIST/PERROT

SUITOR/TOM BLOOD JNR

Note on the Dialogue

A dash (–) at the beginning or end of a line indicates one
line following quickly on from the previous to the point of
interruption at times.

*This text went to press before the end of rehearsals and so may
differ slightly from the play as performed.*

ACT ONE

Scene One

London, 24th April, 1661.

Spotlight on the LADY OF THE BEDCHAMBER, *alluringly dressed, and launching into a patriotic song.*

LADY OF B.

Since the year 1066, there has been quite a long succession,
Of twenty-two kings and a couple of queens, all in line for
    their accession.
Our last, King Charles, with nine kids in all, was
    spectacularly fecund.
Just yesterday his eldest surviving (and some would say
    shapeliest) son was crowned
King Charles the second.

Praise him, praise him,
Praise him.
No other king could be his equal
Brace yourselves for 'Charles – the sequel'
Praise him, praise him.

When he whispers words divine,
His tongue is sweeter than the sweetest wine.
Body of an athlete, hair like a god,
Muscles I could prod and prod.
Taller than I first expected,
Six-foot-two when fully erected.

Love him, hug him,
Squeeze him.
A monarch to unite the nation.
Glory to his restoration.
Praise him, praise him.

*She is holding a used chamberpot which, in her enthusiasm,
she is spilling everywhere.*

As a lover: gentle, kind.
As a boss he speaks his mind.
Quick to finish, long to reign,
I go weak if he remembers my name,
Swearing to serve and not encumber,
Kingly even in his slumber.

Love him, love him,
Looooove him.
He's the best, I daren't dissemble
With one look he can make me tremble.
Stir him, swive him
Raise him, praise him.

*She finishes with a flourish, emptying the last of the
chamberpot with her bow.*

Lights up. We are in the Royal Bedchamber.

KING CHARLES II *is waking up on his bed, half-dressed,
the morning after the night before. Strewn around him on the
bed are a large impressive crown, an orb and sceptre, and
assorted bejewelled trinkets.*

CHARLES. That was noisy, my good Lady of the Bedchamber.

LADY OF B. Your Majesty, pray excuse my vim.

She quivers demurely. Despite his hangover, CHARLES
*exudes youthful vigour in his dark curls and rakish
déshabillé, perhaps set off by a medallion or two.*

CHARLES. I do. And I thank you for getting me up in the
morning...

*He deadpans. Then notices all the Crown Jewels strewn on
his bed.*

That explains the lumpy quality of my sleeping. That and the
historic tumultuousness of my coronation yesterday. God, the
tumult!

LADY OF B. It was good tumult!

CHARLES. Despite ghastly rain, which ruined the fireworks. Anti-royalists say it is a portent. I say it is the opposite –

LADY OF B. An unimportent.

CHARLES. Y-yes, why not. 1661 – what a pretty year! And a numeric palindrome, of course.

LADY OF B. Is it.

CHARLES. Yes. I'm very keen on science.

He stands up, and realises he is still wearing his famous high-heeled golden sandals, making him even taller.

I should have taken these shoes off last night. However did I possess you with them on?

LADY OF B (*suddenly demure*). Oh sir, you must not speak of it!

CHARLES. I have a notion what to do with these Crown Jewels of mine…

LADY OF B. Majesty, your voluptuousness will be the death of me!

She does a lot of coy reacting, averting eyes, etc. He indicates the actual Crown Jewels.

CHARLES. No, these Crown Jewels here.

LADY OF B. Ah yes. An amusing confusion and juxtaposition!

CHARLES. Not for the last time, I wager… As symbols of the restored Right of Kings they must henceforth be kept in COMPLETE and UTTER safety. Where do we place those things we would not have touched?

LADY OF B. I tuck them here down my bodice –

CHARLES. The Tower of London.

LADY OF B. Yes, better, sorry.

CHARLES. We will have them conveyed to that legendary
fortress, a ring of impenetrable steel. But before my beauties
go, let me wear them one last time.

He puts the crown on his head, enjoying the feel of it.

Of course it gives me an extra couple of inches.

LADY OF B. Always helpful. Might I hold one?

CHARLES. Go on then.

*She picks up the bejewelled sceptre, and stands there holding
it, smiling regally.*

LADY OF B. Does this make me your queen?

CHARLES. No. I have a fiancée in Portugal, though I confess
I wed her for her dowry – three hundred and sixty thousand
pounds plus the city of Tangier, which is seemingly in Africa.
(*Wandering off.*) Not now Pepys, you are too early…!

He is gone, leaving the LADY OF THE BEDCHAMBER *in
the spotlight, holding the sceptre like a cheerleader's baton,
completing her song:*

LADY OF B.
Love him, want him,
Have him.
Always utterly iconic
What a man, no what a monarch.
Stir him, swive him.
Raise him, praise him.

Lights out.

Scene Two

London, 1671. A sign appears announcing 'Ten Years Later'…

Lights up on COLONEL THOMAS BLOOD*'s quarters.*

Centrestage is BLOOD, *louche and dangerous.* TOM BLOOD
JNR, CAPTAIN ROBERT PERROT *and* JENNY BLAINE
have just arrived.

BLOOD. So. Hah!

TOM JNR. Hah!

PERROT. Thrice hah!

The men look fired up. JENNY *just stares at them.*

JENNY. Why?

BLOOD. Our enterprise is engaged! We stand at the Gates
   of History with my big idea – to steal from the Tower of
   London the Crown Jewels.

JENNY. What?!

BLOOD. Glittering symbol of majesty, righteousness embodied.

PERROT. Arrant shit!

BLOOD. And how *English* – a hat to show off in. So, the
   present set of royal bilge numbers one crown, an orb thing
   with a cross on it, and three sceptres with bits of gaudy old
   fart stuck in. We shall seize the monarch's crusty cock and
   balls the way they stole my land and the land of my fathers.
   To avenge Ireland, pawed and molested by the English, the
   bastard cuckoos in our nest. You know who you are…

TOM JNR. So you are not at it for the adventure, riches and
   glory, like most else you do?

BLOOD. It is a happy coming-together of enthusiasms. And
   timing: the King shall shortly don these jewels to celebrate
   ten years since his coronation. But the price of failure in this
   enterprise is a swift execution.

JENNY. What?

PERROT. We are not stealing a bunny.

BLOOD. We will not fail. The jewels will all fit in our bag, and
   have the value of three warships. Enough to buy back several

times over my patch of God's gorgeous Ireland before I die – a grand house set in emerald fields, a river to fish in, and a spreading tree to be buried under. My last throw of the dice.

JENNY. I cannot do this – I am an actor! I thought I was here to give a private performance for Tom, who loved me so much in *The Fickle Fool of Falmouth*, in the part of Suki Piss-Quill.

BLOOD. I will come to your purpose soon.

PERROT *empties a flask of spirits into some goblets*.

PERROT. Let us drink to success!

JENNY. It is eight in the morning.

PERROT. Oh let's eat porridge, then, to success! You see how less well it sounds?

JENNY. Do not speak ill of porridge.

TOM JNR. And please be civil to Jenny. She is splendid.

JENNY. Aw, thank ye, Tom.

BLOOD. Nobody is splendid but me, Colonel Blood.

JENNY. My question: would you be so bold were you, rather than Colonel Blood, named Colonel… Jenkins?

BLOOD. The speculation is idle –

JENNY. Or Molesworth? 'Nobody is splendid but me, Colonel Molesworth!'

BLOOD. Are you going to be trouble? So, our stratagem: she and I will to the Tower today in disguise to gain intelligence. Write all this down.

He indicates the blackboard. TOM JNR *picks up the chalk.*

Not Tom! I have another son, Holcroft, who is only ten and already less thick.

TOM JNR (*to* JENNY). My schooling has holes from Daddy dragging us to and fro from Ireland. He having plotted

against the English in Ireland and been discovered, having
before plotted against the English in England and been
discovered. There's been a bunch of plotting.

BLOOD. We came here only because England has no business
being in Ireland yet is AND I HAVE BEEN PLEASED TO
RETURN THE COMPLIMENT. Captain Perrot, write:
Blood and Fake Wife to the Tower to gain Knowledge.

*PERROT does so, with a very heavy hand, and some horrible
squeaking of chalk.*

PERROT. I wish it did not make that noise.

The others agree, muttering to that effect.

BLOOD. Then we men return another day to steal the Crown
Jewels.

PERROT. Death to kings! Death to jewellery!

JENNY. Death to jewellery?

BLOOD. Captain Perrot is a Fifth Monarchist Preacher.

JENNY. What is that?

PERROT. We believe in… fury. And the coming of the fifth
monarch who is Lord Jesus Christ succeeding the Romans,
Greeks, Persians and Assyrians –

JENNY. I regret my question.

PERROT. In all truth I have lapsed somewhat and now work in
silk.

He drinks a shot of spirits, then resumes at the blackboard.

BLOOD. We have much intelligence already. Tom – the book.

*TOM JNR produces a small book from his pocket. He opens
it and reads.*

TOM JNR. '*Handbooke of the Tower of London*. Printed by – '

BLOOD. PAGE EIGHT.

TOM JNR (*flicks to page eight*). 'Fail ye not to pass by the Irish Tower – '

BLOOD. Irish my penis!

TOM JNR. ' – secure citadel of the Crown Jewels which may be viewed upon application to the Master of the Jewel House.'

BLOOD (*repeated, for emphasis*). 'Which may be viewed upon application to the Master of the Jewel House.'

JENNY. So let's away there now. I am in *Hamlet* this evening, and it is very long.

BLOOD. We go when I say so. We need first to fashion a disguise.

PERROT. To what purpose?

JENNY. As an actor I excel at being another, which I can do by face and voice alone. I need no costumery, just some lead-based make-up, and me.

BLOOD. The purpose is to *not be recognised*, ya theatrical wooden-head.

JENNY. Rude.

TOM JNR. Most rude.

BLOOD. What?

TOM JNR. If, like me, you had been at Drury Lane to see Jenny's Fanny Come-Quick you would be as excited as I am. And Jenny assists us out of kindness.

JENNY. And five guineas.

TOM JNR. Granted.

BLOOD. To the disguises.

They help JENNY *empty a sack onto the table, containing wigs, hats, costumes, etc.*

JENNY. Assembled by stealth from theatrical sources. I wore that false leg as Mistress Hopalong in *Marriage Gone Mad*.

They fall on the items like children at a fancy-dress party.
JENNY *is now wearing an eyepatch,* TOM JNR *a huge ruff,*
PERROT *some glittery specs.* BLOOD *puts on a tall clerical
hat. They look at each other, self-conscious.*

PERROT. I fear we look silly.

> BLOOD *adds to his clerical hat a long false beard, held
> against his face.*

BLOOD. I lean towards being a religious man, as they are less
expected to be naughty, despite all evidence. So I choose
these.

TOM JNR. Is the huge beard a solid plan?

BLOOD. Yes – my fame goes far and wide so I need hefty
concealment.

JENNY. 'Far and wide' is an exaggeration, I warrant.

BLOOD. That is because you are an actress so you are daft,
parade before idiots and know nothing.

JENNY (*theatrical intake of breath*). Parade before idiots, is it?

PERROT. Hurrah – a fight!

TOM JNR. Daddy, that was ill-mannered again.

> BLOOD *loses it, drawing his sword and holding the blade to
> his son's throat.*

BLOOD. And who are you, a common highwayman –

TOM JNR. The highways of Berkshire! The pleasant part! And
always politely conducted!

BLOOD. You shame the Blood family with your petty larceny,
– we Bloods stand for things! Freedom from oppression! An
end to colonies! And so on!

Anyone else dare to question me?!

He raises his sword to them all. A scared silence falls.

The devil with planning. Perrot, burn the blackboard. Me and she shall to the Tower to spy the land. Jenny Blaine, choose costuming to play my wife.

JENNY. Wife, or daughter?

The others look away, awkward. BLOOD *twitches with irritation.*

BLOOD. Daughter, say you?

PERROT. Is she too pretty and young for your wife and therefore the ruse would unravel early? Is her meaning. She just called you old.

BLOOD. Thank you.

TOM JNR. Would *niece* perhaps be a happy middle path – ?

BLOOD. Let us worry less about her alleged youthfulness than her performance.

JENNY. Oh I can act, be assured of that. I can do *four* accents. And dance. (*She quickly dances.*) In particular my skill at feigning illness is legendary. (*She quickly feigns illness.*)

BLOOD. That will not be required –

JENNY. Audiences have seen me on stage feigning illness and endeavoured to halt the play all in a panic, I seemed so poorly.

BLOOD. I doubt that, especially if you find the role of my wife so troublesome.

JENNY. Wife it is, then. Easier to pretend it than to be it.

BLOOD. Easier to boast it than to convince us.

Nettled, JENNY *sits on* TOM JNR*'s lap, nestling in lasciviously.*

JENNY. Ooh Tom, easy now, would you. Yes there, right there. Keep doing.

TOM *has frozen, terrified, as* JENNY *groans, building towards an impressive faked orgasm.*

Oooh I am coming apart at the seams. Foh but you will make me splash... Yes! Yes! YESSS!

She finishes with an orgasmic squeak. PERROT *looks faint with arousal at her performance.*

Does that convince...?

Disdainfully rising above it, BLOOD *raises his sword.*

BLOOD. TO THE TOWER!

Lights crash down.

Scene Three

The Tower of London, the Irish Tower.

Modest domestic quarters. There are two pistols on a rack on the wall. Old soldier TALBOT EDWARDS *is having a cup of tea with his jolly wife* MRS EDWARDS.

TALBOT. You know the best item I bought ever? My shiny –

MRS EDWARDS. – shiny boots!

They slurp their tea.

TALBOT. Twenty year and they still –

MRS EDWARDS. – year and they still look like new!

So it's an overfamiliar marriage but a happy one.

TALBOT. Have you dusted the Crown Jewels?

MRS EDWARDS. – Crown Jewels, I have.

TALBOT. Thank ye kindly.

MRS EDWARDS. You can see your face in the stones! But smaller.

TALBOT. – smaller.

MRS EDWARDS. An idea came to me as I was baking: that we offer for purchase to visitors, baked goods in the shape of the royal paraphernalia?!

She shows him a box of misshapen replicas she baked earlier.

TALBOT. I don't understand.

MRS EDWARDS. –stand. Visitors come to see the regalia and you show them, all normal, then you say: 'To solidify the memory of your coming, would you care to buy this sourdough sceptre? A scone orb? Or my yeasty crown?'

TALBOT. And they… take home the cake in the shape of the crown, and eat it?

MRS EDWARDS. Yes, having looked at it for a while, and shown it to their friends, who are intrigued and approving. And they pay more than for a normal cake because it is a celebration of their visit to the Tower of London.

TALBOT *is still struggling with the concept.*

TALBOT. No. Shut your cake box.

MRS EDWARDS. Talbot, the Treasury pays us nothing despite all our entreaties, so we rely on the whim of visitors.

TALBOT. I think it honour enough that we are the King's Keepers of the Jewels.

ELIZABETH, *twenties, drifts in. Her parents look at their ungainly daughter with a slightly desperate love.*

MRS EDWARDS. Elizabeth, my dear, how bonny you look.

TALBOT. Yes.

ELIZABETH. You say such things just to hearten me.

MRS EDWARDS. And we always will, until you are married.

TALBOT. Because we like you. Not to have you gone from our home.

ELIZABETH. That notion had not occurred to me, Daddy!

TALBOT. Oh.

ELIZABETH. Now I am doubting myself.

MRS EDWARDS. Do not.

ELIZABETH. Do not tell me what to feel!

MRS EDWARDS. But that is what we do best.

TALBOT. ...we do best.

ELIZABETH. It's not easy, living in a tower.

TALBOT. 'Tis an honour to live here. Amusing story about honour. I once –

ELIZABETH. YOU SAY AMUSING STORY BUT THEY NEVER AMUSE AND ARE BARELY STORIES. The place is full of prisoners and sinister oddities like wild animals, and bloodstains.

MRS EDWARDS. Elizabeth, I have an exciting thought how you might pass today!

ELIZABETH. Perhaps by making haste to the docks to find me a husband?!

TALBOT. Good plan!

MRS EDWARDS. SHE WAS QUIPPING, DEAR. (*Sweetly.*) Elizabeth! I was thinking rather of you and me making trinkets redolent of the Tower of London which we might sell to visitors, perhaps cakes or tiny replica towers shaped out of dough.

ELIZABETH *makes an adolescent 'Do I have to?' face.*

TALBOT. Amusing story about dough –

ELIZABETH. NO!

A hefty knock on their front door. As TALBOT *quickly dons his official Keeper of the Jewels jacket,* ELIZABETH *stomps off towards an inner door.*

I want to live in a normal place! With no lions in it!

She storms out. Her mother tries to remain positive.

TALBOT *opens the door. Revealing another door of metal bars between him and his visitors:* BLOOD, *now dressed as a curate with a long black beard, and* JENNY.

TALBOT. Good day, and welcome to His Majesty's Jewel House!

BLOOD. Good day to you.

TALBOT. Do you wish to view the royal regalia?

BLOOD. Most keenly.

He and JENNY *are doing painfully friendly faces.* TALBOT *unlocks the grille and lets them in.*

TALBOT. I am Talbot Edwards, Deputy Jewel Master.

MRS EDWARDS. – Master, and I am Mrs Edwards. No official title but I keep a tidy house. So… Mrs Tidy House-Keeper, if you will!

She hands TALBOT *an official ledger and pen.*

TALBOT. Your names, if you please.

BLOOD. Doctor Ayliff, and this is of course my wife.

JENNY. Good day.

MRS EDWARDS. What is your name, dear?

JENNY. Joan.

MRS EDWARDS. How pretty. Like yourself!

JENNY. Thank you. I do the pretty for both of us.

She indicates BLOOD, *and chuckles 'playfully', as do the* EDWARDS. BLOOD *smoulders.*

BLOOD. If I lack lustre it is because she has worn me out since we met, at school.

JENNY. He a schoolmaster, I but a tiny pupil.

TALBOT. I am glad you said it! I was thinking what a singular place of learning, to allow so broad a chasm in ages!

BLOOD *gives* JENNY *a long look. She is smirking.*

MRS EDWARDS. Any children of your own?

JENNY. No –

BLOOD. My wife has no sex organs of any kind.

This silences the EDWARDS; *indeed, everyone.*

JENNY. I do, in fact, aplenty, but my husband does not know where to look. I have explained they are tucked away and less angrily ostentatious than his own –

MRS EDWARDS. Haha! Marriage, the not-so-civil war! – There is no fee to see the precious objects, and the Treasury neglects to recompense us, it being a bad time for money, so if you find your visit pleasant, a gratuity is most acceptable.

BLOOD. I sense already that we will be most satisfied with our time here.

MRS EDWARDS. And what is that by way of a mad accent?!

BLOOD *hesitates. He is doing a shaky English accent.*

BLOOD. I have lived in many exotic places.

MRS EDWARDS. How romantic! You are a curate, by your costuming.

BLOOD. Aye, I live for the glory of God's kingdom, but still have time for earthly beauty such as possessed by the Crown Jewels, and your good self.

MRS EDWARDS *giggles, succumbing to* BLOOD's *charm.*

MRS EDWARDS. Oh, you padres with your honeyed tongues!

She pushes him playfully. BLOOD *pushes her back teasingly.*

BLOOD. Honeyed tongue yourself!

MRS EDWARDS. No, you with your tongue all… honey-fied.

BLOOD (*abruptly businesslike*). How long have you lived inside the Tower?

MRS EDWARDS. Since they remade the regalia when the King was restored to his rightful place.

TALBOT. God bless King Charles!

JENNY. Amen to that!

TALBOT. Amusing story – I met his father once, the previous King Charles.

BLOOD. No!

TALBOT. Yes. Well, witnessed rather than met. In the distance. With his famous pointy beard.

JENNY. That remains sublime and interesting news!

She is massively overacting, as ever. BLOOD *gives her a warning look.*

TALBOT. Charles the first was much shorter than his son. Even before his execution.

MRS EDWARDS. My husband Talbot is a brave old soldier with many a tale to tell!

BLOOD. Ha, yes, but –

TALBOT. I am seventy-seven.

BLOOD. Might we though away to see the jewels – ?

TALBOT. In fact 'twas at his execution that I saw him. Which reduced both his pleasure and mine at the occasion.

MRS EDWARDS. Murder most horrid.

BLOOD. Yes, it was bad.

A solemn moment, which JENNY *interprets as an awkward silence, to be filled.*

JENNY. Boooo.

TALBOT. It is said they stitched his head back on his body.

BLOOD. That was never going to work, was it.

MRS EDWARDS. No no, they didn't believe it would revive him.

BLOOD. Oh I see.

TALBOT. For the neatness of it, I warrant.

BLOOD. Yes –

TALBOT. And lest, the coffin being transported, the head roll about and finish by the feet.

BLOOD. That would be it. Um…?

He clearly wants to get on with the visit, but TALBOT *has a well-worn schtick to get through:*

TALBOT. A word first about the Tower of London himself.

JENNY. The Tower is a *him*?

MRS EDWARDS. Of course, it being proud and sticking up.

TALBOT. Commenced in 1078, it was first a royal residence, therefore William the second, or *Rufus*, him being a ginger, resided here. It was rumoured that he *liked the gentlemen*, partly through *being French*. Since then this place has been and remains the Royal Mint, Treasury, prison, menagerie, much more besides, and latterly home to us Edwards.

During this, BLOOD, *in between nodding receptively, has been surveying the place, casing the joint.*

One famous prisoner, Henry Percy, incarcerated for his doings in the Gunpowder Plot but by all accounts a jolly sort, did install a bowling alley and it is still there, but nobody plays any more –

MRS EDWARDS. – plays any more, take them downstairs to the regalia, Talbot, their ennui is mounting.

TALBOT. Oh. Very well.

He heads for another door, BLOOD *and* JENNY *following, and the three of them head in.*

BLOOD. Though we dearly love your stories…

JENNY. They are not overly long at all…

MRS EDWARDS *watches them go, approving.*

MRS EDWARDS. Her manner is rather over-ripe, but what a nice man.

Scene Four

The Tower of London, the Jewel Room.

A plain room with a cupboard. TALBOT *leads in* BLOOD *and* JENNY, *waffling on…*

TALBOT.…my wife and daughter and I are lucky to live in the best home in London, though 'tis true one hears great groans and cries of distress from the jailhouse close by which *may* be torture but we prefer to think it is a bear or monkey from the King's animal collection.

He has unlocked the cupboard.

BLOOD. How do you know which is the correct key?

TALBOT. Ha-hah!

He taps his nose, and turns back to the cupboard. He recites his aide-mémoire:

Big brass key opens Crown Jewels closet, silver key does safe box deposit.

BLOOD, *unseen, betrays his irritation with* TALBOT, *who now casually pulls back the doors to reveal, with a blaze of light, the Crown Jewels.*

Centrepiece is this Imperial State Crown, made anew for the last coronation and built to endure for many a future King Charles, or whatever kings may be called centuries hence, unless by then people be known only by numbers. Then we have, let me see, this is the Anointing Spoon, so-called because you anoint things with it.

JENNY. Magical. And I love the big ball!

TALBOT. The Sovereign's Orb, which has three hundred and seventy-five pearls, three hundred and sixty-five diamonds, eighteen rubies, nine emeralds, nine sapphires and one amethyst.

JENNY. Might I hold it?

TALBOT. No. Lest you drop it.

JENNY. I will not. I am very good at bowls.

TALBOT. Lest you bowl it then. Or one of the seven hundred and seventy-seven gems fall off or go astray.

JENNY. I promise we are upright and honest citizens.

BLOOD. Dearest, you must understand how wicked folk can be.

JENNY. But my husband is a doctor of divinity and very wise, as befits a man of his great age, notwithstanding his ignorance of my lower workings –

BLOOD. Perhaps you might go and chatter to Mrs Edwards, Jenny – Joanie, Joan.

JENNY. I might, but oh, in truth, I start to feel unwell.

BLOOD. No you do not.

But she goes into her speciality 'feeling ill' acting, histrionic but TALBOT *falls for it. It is obviously not the plan:* BLOOD *looks quietly furious.*

JENNY. Yes, my head spins all about.

TALBOT. Oh dear.

JENNY. And every thing seems unclear.

TALBOT, no fool despite appearances, immediately locks up the cupboard, as JENNY *goes through her acting repertoire. The men watch her, not keen to get involved.*

BLOOD. Might she sit with your wife?

TALBOT. By all means. My wife likes people, whereas I have seen too many cruelties and am not so sure.

BLOOD *steers* JENNY *back towards the door to the* EDWARDS' *quarters*.

Scene Five

The Tower of London, the Irish Tower, domestic quarters.

ELIZABETH *and* MRS EDWARDS *are doing chores as* TALBOT *and* BLOOD *return with a swooning* JENNY.

BLOOD. My wife is swooning.

MRS EDWARDS. Poor little bird! That will be the awe at the jewels.

JENNY. It's not awe, I am ill!

ELIZABETH *is trying to slip away but* BLOOD *is on a charm offensive.*

BLOOD. And you must be the daughter I hear tell of.

ELIZABETH. I am. Elizabeth.

BLOOD. Mellifluous royal name, bravo the Virgin Queen!

ELIZABETH. No, I am named after my dead granny.

BLOOD *pauses: tough crowd.*

BLOOD. Are you married?

ELIZABETH. NO AND I FEEL THE SHAME OF IT EVERY DAY.

She glares at her parents. JENNY, *resenting the loss of attention, groans in renewed pain.*

BLOOD. Forgive my asking, but you are a most attractive gentlewoman with dainty and upstanding parents –

MRS EDWARDS. No stop, YOU are dainty.

BLOOD. – much obliged, but you win the prize for daintiness!

MRS EDWARDS *hits him boisterously, hurting him.*
ELIZABETH *looks mortified.*

I have a young nephew who I feel would be your perfect match.

TALBOT *and* MRS EDWARDS *immediately lose interest in* JENNY *and listen in.*

ELIZABETH. How is he made?

BLOOD. He is most kind.

ELIZABETH. That means ugly.

BLOOD. No, he is sightly with it, with three hundred pounds at his disposal.

ELIZABETH. No that's too fat.

BLOOD. Three hundred pounds a year income in land, which is mine to assign.

TALBOT *and* MRS EDWARDS *instantly abandon* JENNY, *letting her swooning head bang on the table.*

TALBOT. Pray bring him here that he may get to know her.

MRS EDWARDS. And see the Crown Jewels.

BLOOD. I sense Elizabeth will be the real *jewel in the crown* to him.

TALBOT. Does he not have profuse suitors, being so rich, sightly and kind?

BLOOD. Good question. But I know the style of lady he favours and they are very like Elizabeth here.

MRS EDWARDS. *Really?*

BLOOD. Besides, he is full ready to make a family.

ELIZABETH. When might he be here?

BLOOD. Tuesday morning at seven, if that suit.

TALBOT. It does. Why so early?

BLOOD. My nephew… prefers the waking hours, being… an industrious fellow, and loves an early porridge.

JENNY (*calling over*). I am feeling somewhat better now, since you ask.

Nobody cares. BLOOD *heads casually for the two pistols on the wall.*

BLOOD. Are there any other members of the household?

MRS EDWARDS. There would be, but our son Wythe is away soldiering in Flanders.

TALBOT. He is the apple of our eye.

MRS EDWARDS. May he remain safe – our lives would be empty indeed without him.

ELIZABETH *hangs her head in irritation, reminded of her status as least-favourite child.*

ELIZABETH. Agggghhhh…

BLOOD. I like these pistols. Do they fire?

TALBOT. Yes.

BLOOD. May I buy them?

TALBOT (*hesitates*). Oh, um…

BLOOD. I wish to give them as a gift to my aforementioned young nephew. It may sweeten him even more towards your daughter.

MRS EDWARDS. In that case, Talbot…

BLOOD. Good. Shall we say a guinea each?

TALBOT *looks reluctant, as an old soldier, but his wife is looking at him expectantly.*

TALBOT. Very well.

BLOOD *reaches for his purse and pays* TALBOT, *as* MRS
EDWARDS *puts the guns in a bag.*

BLOOD. Are you well again, my dear, so we may leave these
excellent people?

JENNY. In truth no, but I –

BLOOD. Good, what a splendid visit! I look forward to the
next.

He shakes TALBOT's *hand vigorously, and charms* MRS
EDWARDS *by kissing her hand.*

MRS EDWARDS. As do we. Puppy, express your thanks to
Doctor Ayliff.

ELIZABETH. Thank you.

She curtsies, grateful despite herself. As BLOOD, *with the
flourish of a romantic hero, bounds to the open door. Then
remembers he is a vicar.*

BLOOD. Shall I say a prayer? No? Too early?

He makes to leave but realises he has forgotten JENNY, *so
retrieves her, then stops again.*

Forgot the wife. Bless you all!

And he makes a swashbuckling exit, with a well-again
JENNY.

Lights out.

Scene Six

BLOOD's *quarters.*

TOM JNR *and* PERROT *have just been joined by a returning*
BLOOD, *pulling off his disguise, massively excited, which is
bringing out his Irishness.* JENNY *is less fired up.*

BLOOD. It is focking maaad! The Crown Jewels of England are kept in a cupboard guarded by one lunatic auld soldier.

PERROT. Hah!

BLOOD. They are not even vintage, these 'monuments of superstition and idolatry' to quote Oliver Cromwell may he abide for ever in a special hell for what he did in Ireland. I have *cheese* older than these jewels. Nevertheless I want those glittering bastards more than I have wanted anything ever. If only to show that if they are assailable then so is the monarchy and empty entitlement itself.

TOM JNR. Might it not be a wily trap?

BLOOD. How a trap?

TOM JNR. To draw us on, like a donkey lured to a carrot. But a carrot beyond price.

Both men look at TOM JNR, *who is already wishing he hadn't said that.*

PERROT. I am trapped in a room with idiocy.

BLOOD *immediately has* PERROT *round the scruff of the neck.*

BLOOD. No one but me shall pass judgement on my kin.

PERROT. Then I withdraw that observation.

BLOOD. I tell ye, it would be harder work breaking into my actual wife's drawers and making merry with the contents.

PERROT. Have you tried milk thistle?

TOM JNR. Will you please not mention me mammy's undergarments.

BLOOD. I apologise. Little Tom's mother is not well, in fact. But really so, unlike Nell Gwyn here who insisted on doing her *sick acting*.

TOM JNR. I wager you were the most believable unwell lady who ever did live! Like when you gave your Lady Sick-Face in *Five Times a Partridge*.

JENNY. Thank you, Tom Junior. What a pretty review!

She and TOM JNR *are exchanging coquettish looks.*

PERROT. I may heave.

BLOOD. The castle ramparts are attended by guards but they are drowsy and allow traffic to come and go unless alerted otherwise.

PERROT. So when do we do the deed?

JENNY. The question is well asked...

She runs her hand down TOM JNR*'s chest. They growl at each other.* BLOOD *sighs and separates them.*

BLOOD. Tuesday, horrible early.

TOM JNR. Why?

PERROT. When the Tower is quiet.

BLOOD. Correct. Tom, you are to come to marry the fatuous daughter of the Jewel House Keeper, Elizabeth.

TOM JNR (*putting an arm round* JENNY). I would fain not marry her, out of secret personal reasons –

BLOOD. NO THIS IS A RUSE.

TOM JNR. Ah.

BLOOD. To win their trust and distract them, I have bought the old fool's pistols, to deprive him of pistols.

He gets the pistols out of his bag, and brandishes them flamboyantly like a bandit.

In short, my friends, we are set fair –

PERROT. HAH!

BLOOD. Yes –

PERROT. Many times HAH – !

BLOOD. Silence. We are set fair for the greatest robbery in history! On Tuesday at seven o'clock, roughly! The King is about to lose his crown!

Scene Seven

King Charles's Palace, London.

CHARLES *is on a chaise longue, writing a speech, charismatic in wig and semi-regal attire. He has aged visibly after ten years in power.*

CHARLES (*muttering to himself*). Lords and ladies, gentlemen and – women. Youths. My people…

He gets up, and addresses the stalls directly, unnervingly – the theatre his court, the audience his courtiers.

This is a practice, courtiers, for my tenth anniversary speech, which I have penned myself as I pen better than anyone. So if anything in it seems bad, raise your hand and indicate a correction. I find criticism SO bracing.

It's a lie, and everyone knows it, especially his FOOTMAN. CHARLES *reads his speech from a scribbled paper:*

Lords and ladies, gentlemen and – women. Youths. My people. I love you. (*Experimenting.*) I LOVE you. I love YOU. (*To a woman in the audience.*) You in particular, I adore. I haven't seen you before at court – are you with the Rochesters? Or a friend of Squiggly?

Woman in audience starts to reply.

Not you, you look like hard work, next to you. Yes. We got there. (*To the wings.*) Convey the comely woman in blue to me later.

He will continually lapse from his practice speech into the real Charles – sardonic, lubricious, merry.

I stand before you, by the Grace of God, King of England, Scotland, Ireland and France. (*Pause.*) I know, France – something of a hollow boast as we now possess none of it. I had as well be King of Chile, the new long thin country. One thing you should know about me – I love newness. Fresh knowledge. Sinister new foods. And modern clothing – look at me! One thing that is new that I *do not like*, however, is parliamentary democracy.

I resided long years across the Channel while Cromwell occupied my father's purloinèd chair. The most diverting fact about *Crum*, the only one you need linger upon, is that I had him dug up and beheaded. I had sooner done it when he was alive but one takes what one can. His head is still on a pole outside Westminster Hall and offers a pleasant day out for all the family to go and sit on a blanket and enjoy it. (*To* FOOTMAN.) You've done that, haven't you.

FOOTMAN. Yes, Your Majesty!

CHARLES. Did you love it?!

FOOTMAN. I loved it!

CHARLES. But I digress.

He refers to his notes again and resumes, formally:

It is ten bigly glorious years since our God-given monarchy was restored at my coronation, and we may now consider the proud state of our nation. Gaiety abounds. Lady Theatre buzzes and thrives. London is rebuilt after Plague and Great Fire made the middle 1660s so very tiresome. Whatever next, we were thinking as 1667 approached – invasion by Moon-folk? And indeed a bad thing did happen when the Dutch sailed up the Thames and destroyed a fair portion of the English fleet, but we live and learn, and their china and tulips are no longer welcome in our shops.

He goes off-message again:

God, I do loathe the Dutch, don't you? Bruegel?! Bosch?! Shut up! Endless windmills! As we say, or should say: low country, low people. Who do we want to kill?! The Dutch!

Back to his speech:

(*Munificent smile*.) It is a time for kindness and healing. But sedition is an ever-present danger. Religious enmity undermines our natural tolerance – (*To* FOOTMAN.) Is this too heavy?

FOOTMAN. I am fearful of affording an opinion, Your Majesty.

Easily bored, CHARLES *addresses the court/audience again.*

CHARLES (*to someone in the front row*). Hello, where are you from? (*Banter ad lib.*) I... don't know that place. Hello, what do you do? (...) I... don't know that job. Unlike most monarchs, I comprehend common people like you, because when escaping from Cromwell I was pressed full up against commoners while hiding in trees or carts of ox-dung, and once disguised as a washerwoman, a role I excelled in notwithstanding my great tallness, soft hands, and moustache.

He remembers he is supposed to be rehearsing his speech, so scans it, shuffling pages and muttering bits that catch his eye.

Acquired New York... Good lady wife Catherine sadly prone to miscarriages... Unpopular but necessary tax on ovens...

He sighs, too bored to continue.

Enough rehearsal. People of the court, I thank you for your attention, be it real or simulated. By God, I CANNOT WAIT for this celebration of ten years of the restored monarchy when I may wear the Crown Jewels again. They have been kept safe this last decade and I burn to be reunited with them. To become whole again. For what is a king without his crown?

Lights off.

Scene Eight

BLOOD's *quarters.*

Tuesday 9th May. The rising sun shafting in through the window. BLOOD, PERROT *and* TOM JNR *are preparing for the heist, energised. In fact drunk, swigging on flasks. A cock crows.*

PERROT. Confirmation, were it needed, that it is an early hour!

BLOOD. Is everything how it should be?

PERROT. No! Power is falsely apportioned and THE WORD OF OUR LORD IS OFTENTIMES UNHEEDED!

BLOOD. Is everything how it should be for our robbery of the Crown Jewels.

PERROT. Oh, um...?

They check their weapons and clothes. BLOOD *is in his priestly garb but beardless,* PERROT *and* TOM JNR *smartened up, and* PERROT *now has a suspiciously larger gut* (*hiding tools, etc.*).

TOM JNR. Where is my betrothing gift, if I am to play the suitor?

PERROT *tosses him a wrapped gift.*

PERROT. Do not permit your intended to open it.

TOM JNR. Why not?

BLOOD. It is wood shavings.

TOM JNR. Might we not give her a real gift befitting our union? Like a cheeseboard.

BLOOD. We will not be tarrying long enough for pleasantries. We gain entrance, we strike. Sword sticks, Tom?

TOM JNR *hands round the walking sticks. He struggles to pull the blade out of his stick. Taking pity,* BLOOD *tosses his son a bottle of oil.*

Lubricate, for the love of God.

PERROT *and* TOM JNR *snigger blokily.*

PERROT. Lubricate, like a lady...

TOM JNR *lubricates his sword, so it suddenly flies out.*

BLOOD. How on God's earth was he a highwayman...?

PERROT. 'Stand and deliver! No, move on, I have forgot my pistol!'

BLOOD. Enough now, this is a serious day.

A rhythmic banging on the door, clearly an attempt at the code knock. BLOOD *and* PERROT *look at each other queryingly. They mutter gravely at each other:*

PERROT. 'Tis not the knock.

Tension mounts as they draw their swords.

JENNY (*through the door*). WILL YOU LET ME IN OR DO I SET YOUR DOOR ON FIRE?

BLOOD *and* PERROT *look annoyed.* TOM JNR, *relieved, lets* JENNY *in.*

TOM JNR. 'Tis Jenny.

BLOOD. We need you not for our enterprise.

JENNY. I know, I come to say my farewells.

She gives TOM JNR *a massive kiss, and he joins in, the two of them lost in each other.*

PERROT. Will you permit your wife to kiss your son like that?

BLOOD. They appear to have leapt ahead in their affections.

JENNY. Can you blame me, with you taking him off to his doom?

PERROT. NO DOOM! The multitude will celebrate what we do today till the end of the milleniumum... um.

JENNY. Oh dear, you are all very drunk. Is that wise?

TOM JNR. Fret not, my sweet, we are merely fortified against timidity.

JENNY. There is fortified and there is shit-faced.

PERROT. I thank ye to not meddle in men's work.

JENNY. I simply would rather Tom did not hang.

BLOOD. Better to be hanged in glory than creep into our graves. We are none of us imperishable. Anything will put us in our graves soon enough – fire, pestilence, pox, war or bad fish.

PERROT. Or pecked by birds, which killed my daddy. We did not see that coming. True story.

PERROT takes another swig. TOM JNR *is looking worried now.*

TOM JNR. But… we will not be hanged.

BLOOD. NO WE WILL NOT! But if we are, we dangle there –

TOM JNR. Please do not say 'dangle' –

BLOOD. – as lions who did not kneel before the oppressor English. We will be immortal!

JENNY. Though dead –

BLOOD. We will not die, kneel, fail, creep nor dangle, as the jewels are guarded by one old loon and some dozing sentinels, and I am Colonel Blood and my name is legend.

So are we prepared? Tom, who are you?

TOM JNR *(reciting by rote in a Scottish accent).* I am your wealthy nephew doon from the Highlands, wishing with all haste to make a family with Elizabeth.

JENNY. No more of her, 'tis ME ye shall impregnate!

She buries TOM JNR*'s face playfully in her groin.* BLOOD *pulls his son's head away by the hair.*

BLOOD. Work now, play later. And by preference, Tom, not with a woman who feigns to be another person for a living.

He adjusts his priest's hat.

Let us away.

The three men ready themselves, sticks, bags, etc. JENNY *and* TOM JNR *have one last kiss.*

TOM JNR. I do this for you, Jenny!

BLOOD. You do not, you do it for retribution, and a most
   fruitful chaos!

PERROT. So. Hah!

TOM JNR. Hah!

BLOOD. Thrice hah!

The men look fired up, sword sticks at the ready, at the door.

JENNY. No beard this time?

BLOOD. Ah yes.

And they all come back in so BLOOD *can attach his beard.*

Scene Nine

The Tower of London, the Irish Tower, domestic quarters.

TALBOT *and his wife are waiting, he in formal attire,* MRS
EDWARDS *dressed coquettishly for* BLOOD.

TALBOT. I slept as snug as a bug in a rug.

MRS EDWARDS....snug as a bug in a rug.

TALBOT....in a rug.

They sip their coffee.

MRS EDWARDS. However did we wake up before this new
   libation called coffee?

TALBOT. You used to slap me round the face.

MRS EDWARDS. I did. I did do that.

TALBOT. You are dressed most... kittenish for Doctor Ayliff.

MRS EDWARDS. Well he is charming and, when all is said and
   done, I am a woman.

TALBOT. Have you chosen what our Elizabeth will wear?

MRS EDWARDS. Yes, I laid it all out for her. She shared some qualms.

TALBOT. What qualms?

MRS EDWARDS. Whether it made too much showing of her shape, above all her bosom.

TALBOT. She must use every tool in her box.

MRS EDWARDS. – box, amen.

TALBOT. Though I do not want to hear *bosom*.

MRS EDWARDS. Amen.

TALBOT. Amen.

ELIZABETH *enters behind them quietly, half-asleep and not enjoying her dress, which is overly formal but with an eye-catching cleavage. Her parents don't realise she is there.*

MRS EDWARDS. What if Doctor Ayliff's nephew does not want Elizabeth for a spouse? Because let us agree that, unlike our son Wythe, she is not customary in her looks.

TALBOT. No. And she is monstrous peevish.

ELIZABETH *hangs her head – another blow to her self-esteem, already undermined by her clothes. Her parents see her now and are all manic smiles.*

MRS EDWARDS. Ooh, do you look handsome!

TALBOT. Were I not your father I would, you know, phwoar –

ELIZABETH. I HEARD YOU TALKING.

Awkward silence.

TALBOT. Amusing stor–

ELIZABETH. NO!

TALBOT. –ry about talking.

MRS EDWARDS. Dearest, we have a good feeling about this morning and a lemony scowl will not improve your marriage chances.

She grins encouragingly at ELIZABETH, *who softens into a half-smile.*

Now, in case they are delayed, let us set to work making more Tower of London trinkets which we might sell to visitors. What think you of this?

MRS EDWARDS *takes from the oven two large golden balls and a sceptre.* ELIZABETH *and* TALBOT *gaze at the genital cluster.*

Replicas of the sovereign orb, and sceptre, baked gorgeously in pastry.

TALBOT. I am not sure why, but they worry me.

ELIZABETH. BECAUSE THEY LOOK LIKE A MAN'S PRIVATE ORGANS!

She impatiently puts the two balls as far apart as possible.

MRS EDWARDS. Well if you are looking for dirtiness you will always find it.

A knock on the door. The EDWARDS *try to remain calm but quickly descend into agitation,* MRS EDWARDS *vigorously adjusting her daughter's bodice and hair.*

ELIZABETH. Let me alone, Mother – if he wants me, let it be for myself not the whereabouts of my hair and bosom.

So MRS EDWARDS *primps herself, and produces a big fan which she wields.* TALBOT *opens the first door.*

BLOOD, *bearded and dressed as the curate, is on the other side of the metal bars, looking affable.* PERROT *and* TOM JNR *are behind him.*

BLOOD. A blessed and godly good morning to you, sir.

TALBOT. And to you, doctor.

MRS EDWARDS. Also from me.

BLOOD smiles indulgently. ELIZABETH is peering behind BLOOD to get a look at her intended.

We have been so anticipating your return. Where is your nephew?

TOM JNR (*hidden*). Hallo.

TALBOT unlocks the metal bars. BLOOD comes in, followed by PERROT. ELIZABETH's face falls as she sees gnarly, half-cut PERROT, who she and her mother assume is her potential fiancé.

ELIZABETH. Oh...

MRS EDWARDS. Ah...

Then they see TOM JNR and look happier.

ELIZABETH. Ay!

MRS EDWARDS. Haha!

TALBOT. Who do we have here?

PERROT (*remembering his pseudonym*). Cosmo.

TOM JNR. Alan.

MRS EDWARDS. Greetings. And which is your eligible nephew, pray?

ELIZABETH. And we do mean pray.

They look from PERROT to the more marriage-appropriate TOM JNR.

TOM JNR. Och aye!

MRS EDWARDS. Praise be.

ELIZABETH. Huzzah!

TOM JNR. You must be Elizabeth.

MRS EDWARDS. If you don't like what you see – she cooks very well!

ELIZABETH *deadpans*. TOM JNR, *in his Scottish-ish accent, lays on the charm, kissing her hand*.

(*Mutters to* TALBOT.) He's kissed her hand, hand has been kissed…

TOM JNR. She is already good enough to eat.

MRS EDWARDS (*ditto mutter*). A forward compliment, he's paid her a forward compliment…

ELIZABETH (*to* TOM). You eat me first, then I will gobble you.

It's clumsy, and all the men look mildly offended.

PERROT. Not appropriate.

TOM JNR. I have a betrothing present.

BLOOD. Later.

TOM JNR. Oh yes.

But TALBOT, *who has an eye for trouble, is busy scrutinising* PERROT.

PERROT. Hello.

TALBOT. What brings you here?

BLOOD. My parishioner Cosmo desires fervently to see the Crown Jewels.

TALBOT. I smell alcohol.

He looks accusingly at the men. Tension suddenly.

BLOOD. Lingering from last evening. We were celebrating Alan's coming to town.

TALBOT. Uh-huh.

BLOOD. Shall we to the regalia?

TALBOT is still wary but leads them towards the fortified door to the Jewel Room. ELIZABETH grins flirtatiously at TOM JNR.

ELIZABETH. I will wait close by here at the door for your return.

TOM JNR. N- no, do not do that.

BLOOD. You and Mrs Edwards might GO AWAY and make breakfast for us when we emerge.

MRS EDWARDS. A splendid notion.

TALBOT pauses, still suspicious. He looks at the sticks the three visitors are holding.

TALBOT. Why sticks?

PERROT. Shall a man not walk with a stick now?

BLOOD. My friend has bad knees.

TOM JNR. Terrible knees.

TALBOT. I see three sticks. Do you all have bad knees?

BLOOD. No, but we saw him with his stick and… both wanted one.

MRS EDWARDS. My husband has to be careful, in view of his sacred duties.

ELIZABETH. Father is a brave old soldier. We love him all the more for his foibles.

A sweet moment, coming from an easily embarrassed daughter. But BLOOD is losing patience.

BLOOD. To the jewels. They belong to us all, do they not, as the King's subjects?

TALBOT hesitates, his huge ring of keys in his hand, then unlocks the door. Finally TALBOT and the three men are in…

Scene Ten

The Tower of London, the Jewel Room.

TALBOT *leads the three men in. He is back on autopilot, chuntering away as he readies his many keys to unlock the cupboard:*

TALBOT....the Sovereign's Orb has three hundred and seventy-five pearls, three hundred and sixty-five diamonds, eighteen rubies, nine emeralds, nine sapphires and one amethyst.

　BLOOD*'s team are poised to pounce on* TALBOT *but he steps back from the cupboard again...*

　Making a total of seven hundred and seventy-seven gems. Which key is it now...?

　Big brass key opens Crown Jewels closet
　Silver key does safe box deposit... Wait. No...
　Silver key opens Crown Jewels closet...

　The others look impatient. TALBOT *tries a key but it doesn't work. He stops to think again.*

TOM JNR. Can we help – ?

TALBOT. No no.

　He tries a different key but it won't turn. He hesitates.

　I perhaps need to fetch the royal locksmith –

BLOOD. / Not necessary...

PERROT. / Don't do that...

　TALBOT *jiggles the lock dozily.* PERROT *loses it, grabs* TALBOT *and bangs his head against the cupboard.* TOM JNR *throws his jacket over* TALBOT*'s head.* TALBOT *struggles vigorously.*

BLOOD. Easy. Keep your silence and no damage will come to you.

PERROT *pulls from his waistcoat a bag of tools.*

TALBOT. STOP!

TOM JNR *puts his hand over the old man's mouth.* TALBOT *bites* TOM.

TOM JNR. HE BIT ME!

PERROT *and* TALBOT *square up.* PERROT *kicks* TALBOT *in the groin, his knees buckle but he stays bravely on his feet.*

TALBOT (*shouting through his head shroud*). Is that your best!? I have been buffeted harder by wind.

PERROT *pulls the covering off* TALBOT'*s head and shoves a large plug of wood into* TALBOT'*s mouth, restricting him to an outraged gurgle.* PERROT *ties him up, rope round his neck, and goes to quietly lock the door.*

VILLAINY!

They look round to find TALBOT *has taken the plug out of his mouth, so rush over.*

BLOOD. Submit quietly, old soldier, and we will spare you.

PERROT *hits* TALBOT *round the head with a mallet.* TOM JNR *and even* BLOOD *wince.*

TOM JNR. This is too harsh, and pitiless.

To their surprise, TALBOT *continues to make noise.*

TALBOT. The King will not like this...

PERROT *reaches for his stick, withdraws the murderous-looking blade and holds the point to* TALBOT'*s chest.*

PERROT. Will you be shushing now perchance, Methuselah?

TALBOT. No.

PERROT *sinks the blade into* TALBOT*s stomach. He finally slumps to the floor.* BLOOD *and* TOM JNR *look furious.*

TOM JNR. Why did you do that?!

PERROT. So we might go about our business.

TOM *gets down and examines* TALBOT *for signs of life.*

TOM JNR. He is dead, I'll warrant him.

BLOOD. So this is murder now.

PERROT. If they catch us we hang anyway.

TOM JNR. I HATE THIS.

BLOOD. Return to the ladies and assure them all is well.

TOM JNR *winces, not keen, but exits through the door back to the* EDWARDS' *quarters.*

BLOOD *uses the keys to open the cupboard containing the jewels. He grabs the crown and rams it into his bag. It is too big.*

It fits not.

He reaches for a mallet to flatten the crown, and PERROT *thinks about putting the orb down his trousers…*

Scene Eleven

The EDWARDS' *living quarters.*

ELIZABETH *and* MRS EDWARDS *have assembled breakfast and are waiting excitedly for the men's return: They start to open the gift from* TOM JNR *but then* TOM JNR *appears, trying to look composed.*

TOM JNR. Och aye!

ELIZABETH. Hallo!

MRS EDWARDS. They are most fine Crown Jewels, are they not!

TOM JNR. They are. They take the breath away.

MRS EDWARDS. Where is your handsome uncle, and the man with bad knees?

ELIZABETH. Is my father blathering away at them?

TOM JNR. Not so much now.

MRS EDWARDS. Let me serve you some breakfast then.

TOM JNR. No, no thank ye.

MRS EDWARDS. No porridge, your favourite? A *tiny* herring?

TOM JNR. No I am going back in. But I wanted to say 'Och aye!' in the interim.

ELIZABETH. Your hand is bloodied.

TOM notices the blood, from TALBOT*'s bite. He stands there like a rabbit in headlights.*

TOM JNR. Aye. I… bit myself from being so awed by the jewels.

He demonstrates how. A forceful knock on the door makes TOM JNR *jump.*

WYTHE (*through the door*). Open up or I shoot!

MRS EDWARDS (*excitement rather than fear*). Nooooo!

She rushes to open the front door. ELIZABETH *looks happy too.* TOM JNR *is panicking, double-taking between the Jewel House door and the front door.*

WYTHE EDWARDS barrels in – a laughably vigorous, dynamic soldier.

WYTHE. Darling Mother!

He picks up his mother and spins her round athletically.

MRS EDWARDS. Stop now lest my undercarriage end up in the Thames!

WYTHE. Singular sister!

He tries to spin ELIZABETH *round. She resists.*

ELIZABETH. Stop now. I have never liked that.

WYTHE. Where is Father?

TOM JNR. Healthy and laughing, why wouldn't he be?

ELIZABETH. In the Jewel Room with this gentleman's party.

WYTHE realises TOM JNR is there. Thoroughly decent, he offers his hand to TOM JNR.

WYTHE. Forgive me, I am back from battle in Flanders unexpectedly and am overjoyed to see my family.

MRS EDWARDS. We are hoping Alan here will become family too. He is Scottish. We think.

ELIZABETH. Mother, stop! I will decide my own future thank you but a thousand times yes very much so.

WYTHE smiles at TOM JNR, raising eyebrows queryingly.

TOM JNR. Yes, Elizabeth is the one for me!

A metallic grinding and banging drifts through from the Jewel Room. WYTHE's smile dims.

WYTHE. What is that?

TOM JNR. Nothing. But I must go and tell my uncle he has dallied long enough among the jewels, however fascinating.

TOM JNR heads to the Jewel House door.

WYTHE. I will come with you.

TOM JNR. NO! He will reward your father handsomely for his tour, so let us not disturb it betimes. Have a herring.

TOM JNR exits to the Jewel Room. WYTHE's suspicions are aroused.

WYTHE. He seems slippery.

ELIZABETH. Don't care what you think! By St Swithin's Day I shall be married!!

Happier than ever, she jumps deliriously onto his back. And WYTHE notices that the pistols are missing from the wall.

WYTHE. Wait – where are Father's pistols?

MRS EDWARDS (*hand inside the betrothal gift, pulling out…*). Wood shavings!

Scene Twelve

The Tower of London, the Jewel Room.

TOM *rushes in.* BLOOD *and* PERROT *are finishing: the crown flattened and the sceptre cut in half.*

TOM JNR. Their son has returned! Capable. Bouncing. And suspicious.

They hurry to load everything into the bags, as quietly as possible. They head for the other door to the outside, and start to release the mass of bolts and latches on it.

Then realise TALBOT *is on his feet, shockingly still alive, just…*

TALBOT. TREASON! MURDER!

PERROT *stabs* TALBOT *again, making him collapse to the ground – surely dead now. Noise and consternation from the direction of the* EDWARDS' *quarters.*

WYTHE (*through door*). Open up!

BLOOD, PERROT *and* TOM JNR *make their escape.*

The sound of keys being jangled outside the door, a key turning. And WYTHE *rushes in, finds his father stabbed and dying. He hugs him, and sobs.* ELIZABETH *and her mother rush in. Consternation, wordless panic and grief.*

ELIZABETH. What have they done?!

WYTHE *gets to his feet, jaw set, wipes his tears and rushes out in pursuit.*

Scene Thirteen

Ramparts.

A model or map of the Tower of London showing the three men in puppet form escaping with the jewels, slipping easily past sentries, meeting no resistance. WILLIAM *is some distance away with his whinnying horses on the other side of the wall.*

Through morning mist, the real BLOOD, TOM JNR *and* PERROT *appear. But* WYTHE *blocks their way, sword drawn.*

WYTHE. 'Cowards die many times before their deaths, the valiant never taste death but once.'

PERROT. That sounds clever. But is it?

BLOOD. Shakespeare. Like most of the English, inclined to hogwash.

WYTHE. So you are not English.

TOM JNR. Damn.

PERROT. Ah.

WYTHE. Irish, from your peculiar talk.

BLOOD (*fully Irish again*). You are welcome to the information, since you are about to die.

   BLOOD *grins, but bits of Crown Jewels fall out of* TOM JNR*'s bag. As* TOM JNR *bundles them back in,* WYTHE *shouts out to sound the alert:*

WYTHE. The Crown Jewels are stolen! The best of old men is slain!

   ELIZABETH *enters, sword in her hand but obviously no idea how to use it.*

ELIZABETH. I LIKED YOU, AND YOU USED ME! I'll see you on the scaffold instead of at the altar!

They all raise their swords, ready to fight. At which point
BLOOD *pulls out his pistol and levels it at* WYTHE*'s chest,*
poised to fire.

BLOOD. We win, I think. We liberate these toys in the name
of democracy and a fairer world! Ireland first, then other
peoples of the world shall rise up. The end to empty privilege
in all its guises starts now!

Curtain.

Interval.

ACT TWO

Scene One

King Charles's Palace, London.

THE LADY OF THE BEDCHAMBER *appears, reprising her song:*

> Raise him, raise him, raise him.
> Out of bed before his tea time,
> Must be ten year jubilee time.
> Praise him, praise him.
> Praise him, praise him.

CHARLES *joins an ornately dressed* FRENCH NOBLEWOMAN. *As before, he treats the theatre audience like surrounding courtiers.*

CHARLES. I meet a lot of people, remind me who you are.

NOBLEWOMAN (*said in one breath*). Je suis Marie-Françoise Benedicta de Mochefoucauld, femme du Seigneur l'Ambassadeur Français à la cour de Votre aimable Majesté.

A moment.

CHARLES. Oh you're French. I loved France when I lived there. You won't mind having this audience in front of my *entourage*.

NOBLEWOMAN. No.

CHARLES. What I most like about you French is… prithee guess.

NOBLEWOMAN. Our food?

CHARLES. No.

NOBLEWOMAN. Our wine?

CHARLES. No.

NOBLEWOMAN. Philosophers?

CHARLES. No –

NOBLEWOMAN. Our lovely feet?

CHARLES. No –

NOBLEWOMAN. Our cups? Municipal fountains? Our Alps? Montpelier? Limoges? Sheep? Ribbons? The pleasing hexagon-shape of France compared to Great Britain which looks like a witch riding a pig?

CHARLES. You are not Dutch, that is what I like most about the French. (*Pleased with his joke*.) SO. FUNNY. You see, wittier by some distance than a Hollander! Not to mention than Cromwell, who was as amusing as phlegm.

NOBLEWOMAN. All our nations are no doubt a mélange of qualities and blemishes.

CHARLES. Cack! How is my cousin, King Louis? The Fourteenth.

NOBLEWOMAN. He is vey busy! The conclusion of the Treaty of Dover has –

CHARLES. I fear I am too vain to be the fourteenth anything, even the fourth. Does Louis hate being the fourteenth, or does he just not mention it?

NOBLEWOMAN. Eugh –

CHARLES. Do you think you will stop there, at fourteen Louis's?

NOBLEWOMAN. Not if… there are more kings with that name.

CHARLES. I would move on, to King… Raoul? Which is your favourite Louis?

NOBLEWOMAN. Number… fourteen.

CHARLES. Bravo! Quelle diplomate! My favourites are number two, Louis the Stammerer, and number six, Louis the Fat.

NOBLEWOMAN. We French eat well but are not fat. He was perhaps chubby.

CHARLES. Chubby? No, you may be thinking of Louis the Chubby.

NOBLEWOMAN. There was no Louis the Chubby.

CHARLES. Exactly. Louis the Fat was ENORMOUS. I've seen paintings.

He mimes fatness, cheeks blown out, crown on head, big backside, and laughs.

NOBLEWOMAN. Like your Henry the Eighth?

CHARLES *gives her an icy stare, the atmosphere cooling.*

CHARLES. Well it can be very fattening, divorce. Perhaps he ate his wives. Whereas I love women.

NOBLEWOMAN. Yes we 'ave a 'umblesness and 'umanity which –

CHARLES. If I do not lie with a woman every day I become sad.

NOBLEWOMAN. Ah.

CHARLES. Do you become sad without daily congress?

NOBLEWOMAN. No.

CHARLES. How many days before you become sad?

NOBLEWOMAN. Twelve.

CHARLES. Twelve?! Odd fish. What day are you on?

NOBLEWOMAN. Two.

CHARLES. Oh. (*To audience.*) What about you, how many days? Twice a day. Splendid, good work.

(*To the* NOBLEWOMAN.) I urge you, go and see
Cromwell's head on the spike.

NOBLEWOMAN. I will… put it in my diary.

CHARLES. Oh you must – roof of Westminster Hall, take some
friends with you, and a sketching book.

NOBLEWOMAN. How long do you propose to keep the head
there?

CHARLES. As long as whisperers plot against the monarchy,
which I fear will be for ever. I may be the merry monarch but
I approve of an execution, even of an already dead person, if
it is deserved.

NOBLEWOMAN. In France we adore our kings, we would
never chop our king's head off.

CHARLES. The English love their kings too, as you will see
from our impending Ten-Year Jubilee.

NOBLEWOMAN. Yes, I look forward to this. Ten years – the
Tin Jubilee.

CHARLES. Is it. Ah. And you will see me wearing our Crown
Jewels, the best in Europe. I hear the Dutch have just some
cufflinks and a bangle.

His FOOTMAN *approaches, overawed by royalty but keen
as mustard. He waits.*

Speak!

FOOTMAN. Your Majesty, forgive my intrusion but I bring
news.

CHARLES. These news, are they good or bad?

FOOTMAN. I am fearful of affording an opinion.

CHARLES. I am asking for simple intelligence, not a testicle. Is
it Nelly being less insane?

FOOTMAN. No.

CHARLES. Is my new tennis racquet arrived?

FOOTMAN. No, and with respect, Your Majesty, I know
you like to guess but I fear it may take a while. And there
is a lady waiting in your bedchamber, and she has started
whistling.

CHARLES. Good points. Proceed.

FOOTMAN. The royal regalia have been stolen from the Jewel
House in the Tower.

CHARLES maintains a sticky smile, aware of the
NOBLEWOMAN.

CHARLES (*To* NOBLEWOMAN). Shall we end it there? But I
insist you get to know my courtiers – sit among them.

She reluctantly goes and sits down among the audience,
ridiculous in her elaborate costuming.

Do chat with them. Some are amusing though sadly others
are – (*Points to them.*) sly, squalid or dim.

The NOBLEWOMAN *perhaps chats uneasily to the*
audience. CHARLES *turns urgently back to his* FOOTMAN.

So are the Crown Jewels lost?

FOOTMAN. No, all are recovered excepting one or two small
gems which may have rolled away.

CHARLES. God be praised. Else at my ten year jubilee I would
be wearing regalia made of wood.

FOOTMAN. But a crown is bashed flat, the sceptre sawn in
two, and the orb caved in.

CHARLES. Who did it?

FOOTMAN. The fugitive Colonel Thomas Blood, his son and
another, all apprehended.

CHARLES. Then that is most satisfactory.

He has idly taken two tennis balls out of his jacket and been
massaging them in thought, and now gives one a bounce. It
barely rebounds off the ground.

Put tennis balls on the list of things to improve.

FOOTMAN. Yes, sir. You are aware of Colonel Blood, Your Majesty?

CHARLES. As one is aware of a persistent bee in a room, or perhaps better, of *piles*. Blood is a vexatious Irishman who believes that Ireland should be ruled by the Irish.

FOOTMAN. And that is…?

CHARLES. Madness –

FOOTMAN. Madness.

CHARLES (*approaches courtiers*). But there are those at court who believe it. Also, hidden shades, gathering in corners, hard to pick out… Where is Blood now?

FOOTMAN. Retained in the Tower.

CHARLES. Then I look forward to him being tried in court – *very briefly* – and hung.

FOOTMAN. He refuses to speak to anyone but you.

CHARLES. Hah! And I would like a conversation with Our Lord Jesu Christ but it is not allowed me, any more than a money tree or a huge cock.

He realises the FOOTMAN *looks ill-at-ease.*

Yes that is my third allusion within a minute to the private nether parts – I fear my discourse is becoming too earthy. Slap my hand.

He offers the back of his hand for a telling off. The FOOTMAN *really doesn't want to.* CHARLES *rolls his eyes and heads for his courtiers/audience.*

Slap it! I am a king and have been unbecoming. Slap it! Slap it! Fear not, nothing will become of you…

The audience have to be coaxed till someone slaps his hand. CHARLES *looks furious.*

WHAT DID YOU JUST DO!? Do you know who I am? (*Shouted off to a flunky.*) Convey him to the Tower.

Unable to believe it, CHARLES *returns to his* FOOTMAN.

Did you see that?

FOOTMAN. Yes, Your Majesty.

CHARLES. So. How do the people take the news of this attempt?

FOOTMAN. It is not yet widely known. Nor the facts of the robbery, though it seems the royal valuables were not held in very great safe keeping.

CHARLES. Particulars…?

FOOTMAN. The jewels were under protection of an old man, who guarded them alone.

CHARLES. How old?

FOOTMAN. Seventy-seven.

CHARLES. Get out of here!

The FOOTMAN *hesitates, going a bit and coming back, not sure whether he means it.*

Make Blood wait. We will gauge popular sentiment. Also he has friends in court, and *knows things.* Perhaps all the better reason to choke the life out of him and his accomplices within the hour…

FOOTMAN. Shall I send away the lady in your bedchamber?

CHARLES. Never! (*Already heading for her.*) One a day, like apples…

He exits.

(*Heard off, from the wings, to someone else who is waiting.*) Not now, Pepys! I have fleshy business to attend to…

Scene Two

The Tower of London, a prison cell.

BLOOD, TOM JNR *and* PERROT *alone in the fetid cell, manacled to long heavy chains.* TOM JNR*'s head is bandaged. Someone, off, is playing a lament on a recorder or lute, not very well.*

PERROT. WE ARE NOT MINDED TO HEAR MUSIC!

The instrument stops. PERROT *groans, regretting shouting so loudly.*

Eugh… My head is a shithouse. I have a list of regrets longer than these chains. Chief of which is that I did not say to you: thank you but I'll stay here quietly dyeing silk, you go ahead and do the thing that ENDS WITH THE HANGING.

The two BLOODS *are brooding and silent.*

And all so you might buy a fancy house in Ireland with a river and a big tree!

TOM JNR. I will never now fock Jenny.

BLOOD. Moderate your discourse!

TOM JNR. No more of that, aged man. You have killed me.

BLOOD *swiftly overpowers* TOM JNR, *winding a chain round his neck, ready to strangle him.*

BLOOD. I remain in charge, boy.

He releases TOM JNR, *who removes the chains from round his neck.*

PERROT (*quietly, to* TOM JNR). You did not… swive Jenny yet?

TOM JNR. No I did not swive her. She wanted to… 'retain some mystery'.

PERROT. Yes they often say that.

A silence. BLOOD *is still guilty/angry over his son.*

BLOOD. You joined me by your own free will.

TOM JNR. With a bully there is no free will.

BLOOD. We were unlucky, with the return of the lusty son.

PERROT. WHOM YOU, LIKE A BLIND LADY, MANAGED
TO SHOOT AT BUT NOT HIT. His sister, Elizabeth, I
thought well of – I love an angry girl.

TOM JNR. I nearly got away. Life is a slender thing.

He adopts a tragic-hero pose in the shaft of light.

PERROT. Yes, you chose a bad time to fall off a horse.

TOM JNR. I was in a hurry and being pursued.

PERROT. Where was this?

TOM JNR. Gravel Lane, near St Botolph's.

PERROT. You were better to take Hounsditch and go nor-west.

BLOOD. No, better due easterly, through Wapping and avoid
the traffic –

PERROT. Ooh not at that time of the morning.

TOM JNR. Are you done now with the horse talk?! WE ARE
GOING TO DIE!

The horse-boy, William, at least escaped and will have a life.

BLOOD. We will all *have a life*. (*Points to his head*.) I am
working here! You undervalue my resources.

TOM JNR. Oh is that the reward now for killing a man and
failing to steal the Crown Jewels – freedom? Perhaps with a
small gift for the amusement provided?

BLOOD. We shall see.

TOM JNR. I hope they will not try to find Jenny.

BLOOD. You can do better than her. Actors are as reliable as
cats.

PERROT. Yes, my advice: get with a baker, then you always have bread. A lady cobbler is also good, for boots. Potter, same story, pots –

TOM JNR weeps. BLOOD *contemplates his son, goes over and gives him a hug.*

BLOOD. Alright, little Tommy. Whose junior are you?

TOM JNR. Daddy's Tom Junior.

It would be poignant if they didn't have noisy chains round their wrists and ankles, which now get tangled up, needing PERROT *to come over and help. But* PERROT*'s chains get caught up too.*

PERROT. Place your arm underneath through there…

TOM JNR. Daddy, you go backwards…

BLOOD. I never go backwards!

They finally sort it out.

PERROT. I am free!

And the recorder or lute starts up again.

(*Instantly.*) STOP YOUR DISTURBANCE!

He recoils again, hungover.

The sassy woman JAILER *appears on the other side of the bars, musical instrument in hand.*

JAILER. *I* give the orders in this academy of correction.

PERROT. And what power do you have over us? Doomed as we are to await the King's pleasure.

JAILER. Well, since you ask, as your jailer I can kill you. 'Escaping'. Or 'Choking on luncheon.' Or indeed 'Because you were bothersome'.

BLOOD. You are most brave behind your bars.

JAILER. Well bars are traditional, it being a prison. Were it *an hotel* there would be cushions, and I would not be bringing you what I can only describe as shit in a bowl.

She slides three bowls of horrible-looking food into the cell.

PERROT *picks up the bowl and eats, reluctantly, gagging a bit. But then eating with increasing enthusiasm.*

I have a sliver of gossip to sustain you: your blundered exploits are on everyone's lips.

BLOOD. Good.

JAILER. Is it though? You are already flotsam on the waves of public opinion, your reputations no longer in your hands.

PERROT (*as he eats*). Do shut your noise. And pay some respect to Colonel Blood. He is notable.

JAILER. Of course he is. They do not put Billy No-Trousers in the Tower of London. I am no stranger to notorieties like your sorry self, Colonel Blood, and your – (*Consulting paperwork.*) son, I gather, supposedly not so bright –

TOM JNR. My schooling has holes in it from Daddy –.

JAILER. Shut it! And… Captain Parrot.

PERROT. Perr*o*, like *hello*.

JAILER. No, I prefer Parrot like carrot. Yes, luminaries, where you are sitting now we had Sir Walter Raleigh for some thirteen years, before my time but I have read the handbook about the Tower of London.

TOM JNR. / Thank you –

PERROT. / We know it –

JAILER. Wally loved the baccy! And of course the potatoes. Anything from the New World. Pipe in one hand, potato in the other. They say potatoes are not healthy, with all the starch in them, so I take only the tobacco. Then there was Guy Fawkes –

BLOOD. We have read the handbook –

JAILER. – who jumped to his death to avoid being hung, drawn and quartered, so a solid decision really. Pretender to the throne Perkin Warbeck was here –

PERROT. Kill me now…

JAILER. – our only Perkin, to my knowledge. Anne Boleyn. And Lady Jane Grey – because let us not forget the ladies, we are important.

BLOOD, TOM *and* PERROT *are staring at her, glazing over.*

But I fear I have lost my audience, which happens. In any case, you have a visitor.

BLOOD. Whom?

JAILER *(shouting aside)*. VISITOR!

BLOOD. I will not talk to any but King Charles.

JAILER. Can you hear yourself?! Ya big Irish dunce.

BLOOD. They are the King's jewels so I will defend myself to him alone, or is that too complicated for you, ya mucky cockney sloven?

JAILER. He may be too busy organising fair England to listen to you a-whimpering for mercy.

BLOOD. You know me not. I do not whimper.

WYTHE *appears, behind bars, imposing.*

JAILER. Your visitor. The chief visiting rules are: no carnal cupping or coupling through the bars – *(Seeing how angry they all look.)* though I feel we are safe in that regard.

The JAILER *exits.* WYTHE *stares at the three prisoners, eyes boring into them.*

WYTHE. Let me look upon you.

BLOOD *and* PERROT *stand up to him, facing off.* TOM JNR *looks more apologetic.*

TOM JNR. We did not intend to kill your father.

WYTHE. Your intentions were very clear.

PERROT. I regret nothing. He was antique and tiresome and made a horrible din.

BLOOD. Jesus and Mother Mary themselves would have taken turns to stab him.

WYTHE. He is not dead.

PERROT. GOD'S EYELID! How not?

WYTHE. He is a hardy soul, and you cannot even murder properly.

BLOOD. How dare you!

WYTHE. He is sitting up in bed, revived by plans to watch you lose your heads or have them snapped at the neck. He is a hero now, and people shower him with gifts. Cake. Socks. Just now a banana.

BLOOD. What is that?

WYTHE. You will never know. They are new.

TOM JNR. Please give him our best wishes for a full recovery.

WYTHE. I will not.

PERROT. A hearty 'go to Hell' from me.

BLOOD. Tom is right, convey our compliments. If we wished to kill your father, we would have done so.

WYTHE. You are a prick.

PERROT. This is good – we did nothing except nearly steal some jewelled gubbins! And thereby alert our King to the shocking poor state of protection afforded his regalia.

WYTHE. I become more nauseous the longer I listen.

BLOOD. Then why are you here?

WYTHE. To describe to my father, mother and sister Elizabeth the scene before me, of three craven toads.

TOM JNR. Please also convey my best wishes to your sister –

PERROT (to TOM JNR). WILL YOU STOP THIS PANDERING NOW?

TOM JNR. But she seemed so cross. As they say, do not go to sleep on a dispute with a loved one. And I am going on the longest sleep, it would seem.

WYTHE. Indeed you are. Though I almost come to like you.

PERROT. NOBODY GIVES A SILKY TURD.

WYTHE. YOU I like less and less, which I thought not possible.

PERROT *kicks the can of urine, which sprays mainly over the wall.*

PERROT. Have some piss.

WYTHE. It has gone all up your leg.

PERROT. No it has not.

WYTHE. I can see it.

PERROT. No, *you* have piss up your leg.

WYTHE. That is so childish. No I do not.

PERROT. Said by the man with piss up his leg –

BLOOD. STOP, Perrot. You devalue our honourable enterprise with your hotness and poor sense of… everything.

PERROT. I am not hot, I am lively.

BLOOD. FACE THE WALL.

PERROT *looks about to rebel.*

NOW!

PERROT, *cowed, turns to face the wall.* TOM JNR, *growing in dignity, approaches* WYTHE.

TOM JNR. We did use Elizabeth badly, and I hope she finds a husband, if that is what she wants.

WYTHE. No, I fancy that it is pressure from parents and society, and she would rather have herself a little shop selling things. Adieu.

WYTHE *exits.*

TOM JNR. He is right, parents can be like heavy birds which roll over and crush their own eggs.

BLOOD *shakes his head in disbelief.*

But most young prosper, and parents learn their place in the circularity of time. Though my own time is curtailed.

BLOOD. Oh I am not done yet. And I will save you.

It is a sweet moment of bonding. The JAILER *reappears.*

JAILER. Visiting time is over. (*Seeing* PERROT.) What is he doing?

BLOOD. Facing the wall.

JAILER. Why so?

BLOOD. Because I told him to.

WYTHE....he told him to.

PERROT....he told me to.

JAILER. I have word about your fate from the King's people.

BLOOD. What is the word?

Lights out.

Scene Three

In front of the gilded doors of King Charles's Palace. Glorious and light after the jail.

The FOOTMAN, *tray in hand, is mingling with some less-exalted court hangers-on, i.e. the audience. A self-taught working-class boy made good, he is perfectly assured now not in front of* CHARLES.

FOOTMAN. Chestnuts or swan...? Chestnuts or swan...? So the King in deciding whether to grant an audience to Thomas Blood might consider – but will not – that Irish rebels such as

Blood are like orphans, their home garrisoned, with nothing to lose but servitude. Do you take my meaning?

He breaks off to offer his tray of nibbles.

Chestnuts or swan...? But, tipping in Blood's favour, the King hates to be challenged yet then likes it when wearied by sycophancy. Who knows which way he will go. Yesterday he threatened to throw me in jail if I would not honk like a goose all day, then despised me when I did so. By its nature. to be a king is to be one of a kind, and his mind is a mystery.

He does a gesture of hopelessness, and heads off.

Swan? Chestnuts...?

Scene Four

The Tower of London, the Jewel Room.

A month later. TALBOT *returning home, tottering in with his wife. He looks around at what is now effectively a royal souvenir shop. There is a sign 'To the Crowne Jewels* →'

TALBOT. What is this?

MRS EDWARDS. Our Elizabeth has been busy while you were away mending your stomach which was perforated like a colander!

TALBOT. Yes, it was.

MRS EDWARDS. All of London clamours to visit the scene of your valour, so we have left your spilled blood unwashed on the ground, for its special interest.

TALBOT. The red of valiant St George!

MRS EDWARDS. – George, yes, we added paint in a brighter red, as it just looked small and brown. Which prompted questions.

TALBOT. On reflection we should not have kept the Crown Jewels of England loose in a cupboard, but I am not pleased with all this… money-milking. I was honoured with a reward of two hundred pounds!

MRS EDWARDS. Which has not yet been paid, and no doubt never will be, the country being so poor now.

ELIZABETH, *self-assured and wearing a tour guide's uniform, is heard approaching, exiting from the Crown Jewels through the gift shop:*

ELIZABETH.…then he hollered again so the intruders stabbed him in the belly.

TOURIST. No! The worst place! Shabby!

ELIZABETH. Yes. (*Seeing her parents.*) Daddy! Returned!

She runs to put her arms around TALBOT, *which hurts him. With her is a* TOURIST, *a mad-for-it royalist fop, now overcome with excitement at seeing his hero.*

TOURIST. TALBOT EDWARDS! YOU LOOK JUST LIKE YOUR WOODCUT!

MRS EDWARDS. Which can be purchased here!

She produces a souvenir woodcut. The TOURIST *has been looking with awe at* TALBOT.

TOURIST. I'll take it! Forgive me, I lose my speech in the presence of such famousness. Is that a word? How does it feel to be impaled?

MRS EDWARDS. Steady!

General laughter.

I will tell you later.

TALBOT. It feels bad. But I had other things in my head – a big wooden gag!

MRS EDWARDS. Also available for purchase.

TOURIST. I'll take it!

TALBOT. No, namely a mind to protect the Crown Jewels and if necessary die.

ELIZABETH. The scene captured exquisitely on this plate, for three guineas.

She holds up a souvenir plate, of TALBOT *refusing to hand over the crown, being stabbed.*

TOURIST. Oh I do like that. I'll take it! I adore anything royal. My friend and I travelled from Hemel Hempstead to see the coronation. I love your shop.

ELIZABETH. Yes it is the first of its kind. Memories are all very well but you cannot stand a memory on a mantelpiece, or put soup in it.

TOURIST. And word is, you were to marry one of your assailants! (*Sad face.*) *Oh.*

ELIZABETH (*firmly*). No, that is a false rumour. The public are soft in the head for embellished love stories about royal matters and I wish that would stop.

She protests too much. ELIZABETH*'s anger subsides back into her commercial smile.*

TALBOT. Now I and our family are widely feted, Elizabeth will perhaps find a husband more easily. Her qualities are submerged, like good boots in a deep pond.

ELIZABETH. I begin to comprehend why you were stabbed, and with such gusto.

Her parents give ELIZABETH *a look. She glares back, defensively.*

And you should know that I… have a gentleman friend now!

A moment.

TALBOT (*with sympathy*). No you do not…

MRS EDWARDS. – do not, my love…

TALBOT. I need a lie-down. But I live on happily for the day soon when I see Thomas Blood suffer as I did. Hanged first, but half-dead only. Then quartered while still somewhat alive, blood gushing as if from a plashy fountain, till breath gurgles slowly from his wretched partitioned body.

He totters off back to the living quarters, very slowly, watched patiently by the others.

TOURIST. A true hero, if a little sluggish.

MRS EDWARDS. We dare not tell him the King has agreed to give Blood an audience.

ELIZABETH. It is merely the prologue to his execution. So! So you've seen the regalia, exquisite and unique. And reproduced here! For three guineas in iron, or two shillings in pastry. Pastry? Iron? Iron? Pastry? One of each?

TOURIST. Pastry?

ELIZABETH. Good choice. As iron would have been.

MRS EDWARDS *racks his purchases up on the abacus.*

MRS EDWARDS. So that is: one woodcut, a painted plate, a bowl showing the King holding a lamb, ornamental wooden gag, and a pastry Crown Jewels. Eight guineas, and a groat for the bag.

As the TOURIST *pays, a handsome young uniformed* SUITOR *has entered, unannounced. Concern in the room as to who he is. But he and* ELIZABETH *are walking towards each other.*

SUITOR. Elizabeth…

ELIZABETH. Martin…

SUITOR. I am come!

He kisses her hand, fervently but with great respect. The couple look round to see MRS EDWARDS *gazing in disbelief.*

ELIZABETH. This is Captain Beckman. We met lately at a dance to raise money for victims of bad things which have happened.

The SUITOR *does a deep bow to* MRS EDWARDS.

SUITOR. Mrs Edwards, might I ask for your daughter's hand in marriage?

MRS EDWARDS *is too shocked to react then, along with everyone else, breaks into a tearfully emotional grin.*

TALBOT (*off*). At last!

Lights out.

Scene Five

King Charles's Palace, London.

CHARLES *approaches, having a final practice of his speech, pen in hand to make corrections, skimming through it.*

CHARLES. Ten years of marriage to esteemed but infecund consort, Queen Catherine… So love my people… pleased to wash the feet of the poor… (*To self.*) despite a toenail once coming off in my hand, best not say that, hazards of the job.

Obviously bored by his speech, he calls to his FOOTMAN.

Bring me a bowl of cream ice. With the other new thing, a… nabana?

FOOTMAN. A banana.

CHARLES. Abanaba?

FOOTMAN. No, banana.

CHARLES. Nobbanaba?

FOOTMAN. Banana.

CHARLES. Banana. Too much to learn. I should have lived in the Middle Ages, when the world stood still.

The FOOTMAN *exits and* CHARLES *turns back to the speech, finding something he is more interested in, sharing it with the audience.*

Ah yes, something more stirring: an attempt to steal the Crown Jewels has been defeated by brave compatriots. What greater fymbol– (*Peers at script.*) symbol of our now most solid monarchy!

He is warming to his theme, becoming Churchillian, improvising theatrically:

This crown and other... jewelled appliances are more than mere gold and bijous, they are... the very hats and spheres of civilisate-y-on, for they glister brighter than one thousand stars... than one million stars...

The FOOTMAN *returns, carrying on a tray a bowl of ice cream and a bunch of bananas.*

FOOTMAN. Your cream ice, Your Majesty.

CHARLES. What comes after one million?

FOOTMAN. You do not mean two million?

CHARLES. Of course I don't. I know there have been daft kings – Louis the Daft, probably, and others – but I am not one.

FOOTMAN. Forgive me. I believe the word 'billion' is finding favour, over from France. It means a million times a million.

CHARLES. That is quite a jump.

FOOTMAN. Yes. Your Majesty.

CHARLES (*trying the ice cream*). Ooh very good. Also from France, like the billion thing?

FOOTMAN. Yes, Majesty.

CHARLES. Pity. But at least not from the Netherlands, where they could not invent an arsehole if you gave them one in a box, with instructions!

FOOTMAN. Indeed not, sir. Colonel Blood is still without.

CHARLES. Then fetch him in to sing for his life. Then we
execute him anyway, lest a line build up outside the Tower of
other desperados with the same intention. I only hope he is
amusing, or truculent, rather then tearful.

The FOOTMAN *has already gone.* CHARLES *picks up his
bowl of ice cream and eats, enthusiastically.*

(*To the audience.*) Mm, do try this when you can. Most
refreshing. Very good in a warm theatre, say.

He shovels ice cream in as BLOOD *is led in, chained,
escorted by the* FOOTMAN *and a* GUARD. BLOOD
and CHARLES *gaze at each other, then* BLOOD *does an
elaborate bow.*

BLOOD. My most glorious sovereign, I am your obedient
servant.

CHARLES. But you are not, are you. You are many adjectives –
greedy, deceitful, Irish, chained, doomed – but not obedient.
Aagghh my brain! Cold and achy!

He clutches his head. BLOOD *and* GUARD *look confused.*

FOOTMAN. I fear it is the cream ice, Your Majesty.

CHARLES. OH, DO YOU THINK SO?!

*He holds his head still, waiting for the pain to ebb, which it
does.*

I perhaps ate it too quickly. Good. So, Colonel Thomas
Blood – not a real colonel, I am told, but that is the least of
your delusions – we meet in person.

BLOOD. Yes, my Liege. Thank you for admitting me.

CHARLES. Well it seems nobody else is good enough for you.

BLOOD. I wish to explain in person my motives.

CHARLES. I bet you do. There will be surprise abroad that I am
deigning to see you.

BLOOD. We rise above such surprise, do we not?

CHARLES. Do not bracket me with you.

He gazes icily at BLOOD.

BLOOD. We rise above it from very different positions…

CHARLES. Precisely. But first some niceties, as we are not savages, well I am not – we have acquaintances in common.

BLOOD. We do?

CHARLES. The Duke of Ormond whom last year you kidnapped, took away on horseback and tried to hang at Tyburn.

BLOOD. That was not me.

CHARLES. Do not lie, else I will terminate this and have you dead within the hour.

BLOOD. I was responsible, and applaud any attempt on that pig the Duke of Ormond's life, but I was not there doing it. Or it would have gone off successfully.

CHARLES. Did the theft of the Crown Jewels *go off* successfully for your being there?

BLOOD. No –

CHARLES. You say you wish to explain your motives, yet I have abundant reports on them already, in these publications.

He indicates a pile of newspapers, including the London Gazette, *pamphlets, posters, etc.*

Which must be sweet music to you – you are a dog for fame, are you not?

BLOOD. We all, or mostly, deserve our day in the sun. So many must live shaded by lesser souls, your majestic self excluded.

CHARLES. Well done. Indeed. There are even poems being writ about you.

BLOOD. And now I *am* anxious. We Irish take our poetry seriously.

CHARLES *picks up a piece of paper.*

CHARLES. Let us see. The celebrated Andrew Marvell offers us:

'When daring Blood his rent to have regained
Upon the Royal Diadem distrained.'

The two men, and the FOOTMAN *and* GUARD, *look blank, not getting it, or not impressed.*

'He chose the cassock, surcingle and gown
The fittest mask for those who rob the Crown.'

Better.

BLOOD. Yes, I understand that bit.

CHARLES. 'But his lay pity-underneath prevailed
And while he sav'd the Keeper's life, he failed
Within the Priest's vestments had he but put
Bishop's cruelty, the Crown was gone.'

The men look perplexed again.

Dreadful nonsense.

CHARLES *scrunches the poem up and tosses it away. He reaches for the newspaper.*

The *London Gazette*, a putrid organ be it said, reported: 'Notorious villain Colonel Blood…' Prithee don't rattle your shackles while I am talking.

BLOOD *holds up his hands noisily in apology and stands still.*

'Notorious villain Colonel Blood, assisted by half a dozen knaves, and a woman with them, did storm the Tower.'

BLOOD. A lie.

CHARLES. Which?

BLOOD. Every particular.

CHARLES. Oh bad luck. Something is usually correct in a newspaper, if only by chance. (*Laughs at length.*) So. Funny.

BLOOD. We were three people only.

CHARLES. Plus your accomplices – a horseman, and the woman on your preliminary visit, who acted as your wife though considerable younger than you.

BLOOD. A trait we share, then.

CHARLES looks shocked at BLOOD*'s bold reference to his mistresses.*

CHARLES. What are the names of your little helpers?

BLOOD. I will not say. I have my honour still, and this tiny adventure was my idea not theirs.

CHARLES. We know who they are: Jenny Blaine, an actor, and William Smith. We know everything.

BLOOD. Then you know that I robbed the Crown Jewels not to injure you but to strike a little blow for Ireland, that most wronged place.

CHARLES. It is not *wronged*, it is *owned* and *improved*. As Rome *owned* and *improved* Britain, first loathed for it then loved, as Ireland, and all our colonies, will love Britain in time. So that was treasonous. I am merciful but have my kingly duties. Take him away and execute him.

The FOOTMAN *moves towards* BLOOD*, who looks relaxed.* BLOOD*'s eyes have been drawn to* CHARLES*'s tray of refreshments.*

BLOOD. Before I *head off* – haha – is that one of the new bananas?

CHARLES. No, it is called a… Yes it is.

BLOOD. As my last request, might I try it?

CHARLES. Why?

BLOOD. Long story.

CHARLES. With a short answer: no. I am not a grocer.

BLOOD. Does it taste like a lemon? Both being yellow.

BLOOD *nods, smiling cheekily at* CHARLES, *which disarms the monarch.*

CHARLES. No. It is more clammy. (*To the* FOOTMAN.) Is it not?

FOOTMAN. Yes, like a plum encountering custard.

BLOOD. Thank you. While I am still here, as to Ireland, I meant 'wronged' not by Your Majesty but by loathèd Cromwell, repository of evil. He killed your father then murdered my country.

CHARLES *weighs* BLOOD *up, and indulges him a little longer.*

CHARLES. Then we agree on something. I have put his head on a pole, you know.

BLOOD. I do. It is my favourite attraction in London. I admit also that I needed the money. Your Majesty is no stranger to pecuniary hardship, running as you do a country held together with borrowings like a battered barn.

CHARLES. Also true.

BLOOD. So jewels valued at some one hundred thousand pounds, and stored in a closet guarded by a forgetful pensioner, were a temptation too succulent to resist.

CHARLES. Then know that their value was six thousand pounds.

BLOOD. Only six fecking thousand?! That's fraud!

CHARLES. Truly no one is more prone to moralising than a criminal.

BLOOD. So worth not even half a warship, rather than three, as rumoured.

CHARLES. Was your plan to buy a warship with your gains?

BLOOD. One never knows where the whimsy takes one.

CHARLES *is amused, more relaxed now.*

CHARLES. I asked in my circle for opinions on you. Half offered to hang you themselves as a man utterly without principle. The other half were inclined to indulge you for your occasional endorsement of the monarchy.

BLOOD. Well it is no secret now that I admire and covet royal trappings. On which subject, please forgive me for flattening the crown and sawing up the... long thing.

CHARLES. I am told they can be plumped up again and stuck together, in time.

BLOOD. Good. As to royalty, I admit I have changed sides before in search of the democratic ideal – Anarchism *so nearly right* but probably exhausting in the long run. But I have now concluded we are best served by a monarch we can trust to employ their power responsibly, and wear a coronet with panache, as you do.

CHARLES. Your chosen weapon of defence, then, is candour tempered with roguery and a thin layer of flattery. Do you presume that is enough to save you?

BLOOD. You have seen enough bloodshed, and I am no use to you dead.

CHARLES. Nor alive.

BLOOD. On the contrary – spare me and I am your eyes and ears. Our little secret. I know every Irish assassin, every London cabal. Kill me, and you will summon to the cause every rabid dissenter looking for motive to do you harm.

CHARLES *ponders, pacing. He idly tosses the banana to* BLOOD, *who bites into it whole.*

FOOTMAN (*mutters to* BLOOD). It is eaten with the skin off.

BLOOD. That explains it.

He gingerly takes the skin out of his mouth and eats the actually banana, loving it.

Mm, dainty. Custard is coming through. Before you pass judgement, might I do a dangerous thing?

CHARLES. Another one?

BLOOD. And suggest that you and I are indeed kindred souls.
We both love an escapade. Like me you have hid in trees…

CHARLES. So many trees…

BLOOD. – and tasted exile, and been driven by lunatic
enthusiasms: knowledge!

CHARLES. Knowledge!

BLOOD. Fathering children!

CHARLES. Fathering!

BLOOD. Racehorses!

CHARLES. Racehorses!

BLOOD. WOMEN!

CHARLES. WOMEN!

BLOOD. I love all that in a man!

CHARLES. YES. IT'S GOOD!

BLOOD. Your Majesty, I feel I know you, let me guess what
you are thinking.

CHARLES. I LOVE A GUESSING GAME!

BLOOD. You are thinking: I am a king, my life should be less
cruel and more kind.

CHARLES. No I was not thinking that –

BLOOD. Then you were thinking –

CHARLES. Enough talking, I have made up my mind.

The mercurial despot again, he stares at BLOOD, *who looks
tense.*

Lights out.

Scene Six

The LADY OF THE BEDCHAMBER *appears, clears her throat preparing to sing a wayward but heartfelt ballad.*

LADY OF B. I have wrote a ballad. For voice, and orchestra.

She produces perhaps a small drum, and/or introduces a lone musician with an instrument.

Oh listen carefully would ye,
To my terrible, terrible song.
It's a ballad of heroes and bravery,
Daring deeds and a crime that goes wrong.

Talbot Edwards prevented the robbery.
Now the veteran's a legend to all.
He was old, he was lame, he was doddery
Truth to tell he'd had more than one fall.
Though stabbed and speared, and dying they feared,
When the treasonous felons did flee...

*He sang 'Diggle oh diggle down dilly
Diggle diggle oh diggle down dee.'*

If you're asking 'What could have convinced her
That the traitor was better off dead?'
There's a spike on a wall at Westminster
Calling out for one Colonel Blood's head.
And if his gang, were set to hang
Would that fill me with dread and dismay?

*I'd sing 'Diggle oh diggle down dilly
Diggle diggle oh diggle down day.'*

She stretches the tension by slowing down the tempo, less larky now.

And once they're flayed, and deceased and displayed,
When they're no more than food for a crow.
Would we feel any guilt? Don't be silly.
We'd sing 'Diggle oh diggle diggle down doh.'

Lights out.

Scene Seven

Grassland.

Morning mist, lit by the sun. It looks unreal and paradisal, as though this may be Heaven.

Out of the sun strolls a serene BLOOD, *dressed in best Irish laird clothing. He gazes around. Birdsong.*

BLOOD. How focking delightful.

> TOM JNR *joins him. Their relationship is more affectionate and equal than before. They stand there contentedly. Noise of a sheep, then a cow. And in the distance a country house appears as the mist clears.*

TOM JNR.So this is what Heaven looks like.

BLOOD. If Heaven looks like County Kildare. Always a possibility.

TOM JNR. I struggle still to know how we are alive.

BLOOD. Because I argue well, and leak charm at will like those cows leak milk.

TOM JNR. The pardon I understand, though with difficulty, but to be given an Irish estate and pension seems perverse.

BLOOD. Even a king needs friends, for what is a royal house but a band of naughty miscreants bent on survival. And I serve him very well, when I can be bothered.

> *He gets a pipe out and starts smoking.*

Also everyone loves a story, if it is a good one. Otherwise what are we, Tom – mere rutting animals wading through formless lives.

TOM JNR. If the old soldier had died, they would be less forgiving.

BLOOD. Perhaps. But history is nice with the details. As long as we did not kill a cherished pet dog, them being English, we had chances of indulgence.

TOM JNR. Some are angry that we still breathe, even before the addition of gifts and an estate with cows.

BLOOD. Well some are always angry, at everything. *I* was. The King had in mind to show leniency to the newly benign. Which I am glad to be, as age makes me practical. I had heroism in me, but not always the best kind. And I am happy to spy and whisper at court against the new generation of tiresome Irish and other hotheads.

Amused, TOM JNR *looks at his father as he smokes his pipe, and down at his feet.*

TOM JNR. The ferocious wordy renegade is wearing slippers.

BLOOD. They are pleasantly forgiving. Like my mind now. We think too much of nations. They are moonshine. Belonging comes in better shapes – tranquility shared, kinship.

A moment between them.

TOM JNR. I remember that day as one does a dream. Full of wild moments, and being chased after, then I woke up and it was all a reality.

BLOOD. Mm.

TOM JNR. What news of Captain Perrot?

BLOOD. He *does* remain fully angry. He is asking for a share of my pension, which I will not give him.

A sheep baas.

Though I will send him a sheep for his birthday.

A cow moos.

Or half a cow.

TOM JNR. He was not easy company, but we were all foolish.

BLOOD. You are young – you still have plenty of fool in you.

TOM JNR. No, I am reformed, given up the highwaymanning. Looking for honest work, perhaps in fashion.

BLOOD (*nods, not unhappy*). Fashion. Whatever happened to Jenny?

TOM JNR. She… (*He turns.*) stopped to puke behind a tree – there she is.

JENNY enters. She is very pregnant. She puts her arm lovingly in TOM JNR*'s, and looks around.*

JENNY. Oh it's frigging gorgeous.

The men nod. They all gaze at the gorgeousness, then JENNY *looks alarmed, then in pain.*

Ah it is starting. I feel it.

She groans and doubles up. TOM JNR *looks concerned, immediately panicking.*

TOM JNR. The baby! I'll go fetch the doctor. SHALL I?

JENNY. Too late!

TOM JNR. THEN, GOOD, NO, I WILL STAY HERE AND HELP! BY… DOING THIS. IS THAT HELPFUL?!

TOM JNR *clumsily helps* JENNY *get comfortable, as she gets on all fours and breathes hard.* TOM JNR *realises his father is still calmly smoking his pipe, unconcerned.*

TOM JNR. FATHER!

BLOOD. She is acting.

JENNY. I am. I am only at six months. Keep up.

She straightens up, perfectly well. A moment, then TOM JNR *looks amused and delighted.*

TOM JNR. Aagghh. Again!

JENNY. Ah, I love a credulous audience. We will be very happy here, and finally settled.

The three of them stand there, happy. Irish pipes fade in.

BLOOD. After we take the boat from Dublin this evening, to attend our friend's party.

TOM JNR. Must we?

BLOOD. It is not a friend one says no to…

Scene Eight

A palace.

CHARLES, *dressed in official finery and wearing or holding all the Crown Jewels, is giving the speech he's been rehearsing throughout the play. Gathered alongside him in their finery are the* FOOTMAN, NOBLEWOMAN, *and our* TOURIST, *who looks ecstatic to be there, wearing royalist accessories bought in the Tower shop.*

CHARLES.…and as we assemble to celebrate this landmark of the coronation, somewhat delayed by repairs being needed to these (*Indicates the Crown Jewels.*) it is hard not to think of the other King Charles. His reign cruelly shortened by circumstances.

A murmur of agreement, some 'Hear-hears' – a sense of a large crowd gathered to listen.

His body also cruelly shortened… But it is a time for looking forward. Another king, Henry, the Fourth, quoth: 'Uneasy lies the head that wears the crown.'

He theatrically indicates his crown.

But let us rejoice that there is a crown to wear, and a golden orb to hold, and a sceptre to… wave. The recent attempt to steal our regal paraphernalia has reminded us all that these are more than heavy shiny objects, they are talismen for our future. Welcome, our friends.

The assembled are joined by a smartly dressed BLOOD, TOM JNR *and pregnant* JENNY…

So will you be upstanding and raise a glass.

He raises a goblet, and gestures to the audience – ours as well as 'his' – to stand.

Imagine a glass if you have none, don't make this difficult. If you are *actually* not able to stand then I will give you the benefit. Usher, put that lady on her feet, she is just being lazy. (*To a pretty audience member:*) You I am seeing afterwards, yes? And you too, why not?

The audience are now on their feet, hopefully.

You will say with me this poem I have written to celebrate the Crown Jewels*:*

C… is for Crown and Charles and Celebrant
(*Repeating slowly.*) *C* is for Crown and Charles and
   Celebrant
R… is for Regal, Royal, *Re*splen-dent
(*Slowly.*) *R* is for Regal, Royal…

The audience are struggling, trying to speak along with him, but it's a mess.

Stop, stop, this is a coach crash. I will proceed alone, on foot. But you may join in with the remaining first letters only of *Crown Jewels,* which I hope you know.

O… the shape of wonder our mouths do spell
W… what-a-thing we do so well!
N… None for pomp is e'er our parallel.

J… is Jewels, like Great Britain all a-gleam
E… lizabeth, best queen there's ever been.
W… for Wisdom, may I achieve
E… lizabeth, again, my model to succeed.
L… ove me pray, your merry monarch Charlie
S… o keep your hands off my Crown Jewels entirely.

In celebration he brandishes his sceptre and holds his orb.

Finally, to cement our sense of national pride, I am instigating what shall be called a National Anthem, which my former Lady of the Bedchamber, now Head of Music, will lead us in.

His former LADY OF THE BEDCHAMBER, *now grander and more akin to the helmeted warrior Britannia, comes forward. Incorporating the curtain call, she sings a rousing national anthem – what 'God Save the King' should be – with our full cast joining in on the jingoistic chorus verses.*

LADY OF B.

Oui, oui, oui, how we love our glorious land.

Aye, aye, I feel my jutting breast expand.

Si, si, see how we sing with all our might.

Hai, hai, hai, high and loud throughout the night.

We're not French, nor Dutch, God knows. We're nothing like the Spanish.

We subjugate and tame our foes, and those we loathe we banish.

Norwegian we're not, nor Danish no! We're surely not Italian.

We dominate where'er we go, with our immense battalion.

ALL. Dog, dog, dog not our footsteps with your gloom!

Hoarse, hoarse, hoarse! Are our throats, as voices boom.

Trump, trump, trump, trumpets sound, the lute it thrums.

Bing, bang, bong! There they go – our big old drums!

LADY OF B.

The Turks and the Greeks are not unique in causing repercussions.

We find the Germans rather bleak, and don't get along with Russians.

We're tolerant to foreigners, we haven't a vendetta.

Those other nations are all fine, but we are simply better.

ALL. We are simply better.

Fork, fork, fork! With Britannia's trident prongs.

Toss, toss, toss! Our opponents weak or strong.

No, no, no, never fail, no ifs nor buts!

Yes, yes, yes! We have such enormous guts!

Charge, charge, charge, charge your glasses, sound the gong.

Toast, toast, toast our anthemic national song.

No, no, no, We can't help it if we're blessed!
Yes, yes, yes! We're just better than the rest!

LADY OF B.

Yes, yes, yes! We are better than the reeeeeeEST!

ALL. – cleverer, nicer, prettier, wiser, braver, better-err...
BEST!

Curtain.

The End.